CITIZENS IN THE PRESENT

CITIZENS IN THE PRESENT

Youth Civic Engagement in the Americas

MARIA DE LOS ANGELES TORRES
IRENE RIZZINI
NORMA DEL RÍO

UNIVERSITY OF ILLINOIS PRESS
URBANA, CHICAGO, AND SPRINGFIELD

Library of Congress Control Number: 2013938955

In Memory of Harold Richman and Pastora San Juan Cafferty
And with Special Appreciation
to Matthew Piers, Malcolm Bush, and Ignacio Durán

The two antagonistic forces of past and future are both indefinite as to their origin; seen from the viewpoint of the present in the middle, the one comes from an infinite past and the other from an infinite future. But though they have no known beginning, they have a terminal ending, the point at which they meet and clash, which is the present.
—Hannah Arendt, "Thinking"

Hold to the now, the here, through which all future plunges to the past.
—James Joyce, *Ulysses*

Contents

Illustrations

Preface

As we finished this manuscript in the spring of 2012, young people were back on the front pages of political news. From the Arab Spring uprisings to the pro-immigrant marches throughout the world to the Occupy Wall Street movements—to name a few—young people have become protagonists of protest movements and efforts to find alternative ways of thinking about equality, inclusiveness, and fairness in a globalizing world. Many have moved outside traditional forms of political activism to engage in nontraditional arenas—many of them private—that influence their lives.

Who are these young activists? What influenced them to step out of their private lives and engage in public battles? If forms of traditional democratic practices were being undermined by a rapidly accelerating unequal distribution of wealth and power and its consequences on the blurring of private/public spaces, how do they engage to effectively influence institutions in urban spaces—increasingly becoming the place for the majority of young people in the world—that affect their lives? And what are their ideas about politics? Our study aimed to understand the trajectories of youth activists. We recorded the narratives of young people working to improve their lives and their neighborhoods in three global cities. As such it is a book about how they became engaged, what kinds of activities they pursued, and how they envisioned their world.

Our perspective is interdisciplinary, and as such the questions that guided our project came from our respective fields; psychology, sociology, and political science. Early childhood influences are critical to the well-being of young adults; do they also influence political behavior in later lives? How do young people identify their collective selves and how do they mobilize? What are the philosophical underpinnings of how young adults envision their world, their place, and government's role in it?

The sites of our study were global cities in the Americas; while each city has a very distinct history and political culture, collectively these cities allowed us to engage in a hemispheric comparative exercise that gave as an opportunity to search for commonalities and differences.

We shared a deep respect for young activists and a desire to understand their contributions to the broader questions of civic engagement, personal responsibilities, and the state of democracies in these global cities. As Hannah Arendt so aptly observed, the political is where individuals come together to create futures. It is precisely in political action that the collective is forged and authoritarianism is checked. Even though she was leery of placing children at the forefronts of political struggles, the young people with whom we worked were adolescents and young adults keenly aware of how they were constructed in the media, excluded from the public, and marginalized from the communal polity. They made informed decisions to engage in battles that could let them have an effective voice in decisions that affected their lives and their communities. In the process, they forged new and meaningful political identities.

At the core of our project is also a deep concern about the viability of democracies given the deep inequalities that characterize contemporary societies that are starkly visible in global cities.

Democracies cannot provide citizens with a formal public voice without ensuring some level of equality in the private realm that allows individuals to have an equal footing in institutions that have power over the public realm. Could the practices and ideas of young activists suggest new ways of rethinking democracy and its practices in the age of globalization? We explore these concerns through the narratives of the young people who trusted us with their experiences.

Acknowledgments

It was through Harold Richman that this project became a reality. His life-long commitment to research and advocacy on behalf of youth around the world helped inspire this project. It is to his memory that we dedicate this book. His invitation to Maria de los Angeles Torres to spend a year as a fellow at Chapin Hall allowed her to develop this project. Through him, Irene Rizzini was introduced to the project, and she in turn brought Norma Del Río. Very special thanks to Pastora San Juan Cafferty, who made the initial introductions and was a lifelong mentor and friend.

At Chapin Hall, Mark Courtney enthusiastically supported our project—as did Ada Skyles and Robert Chaskin. Miguel Satut, formerly of the Kellogg Foundation, generously supported our efforts, facilitated our meetings, and made possible the three youth publications that emerged from our interviews. Irene Rizzini held two fellowships during the course of the work that greatly aided her participation: the visiting chair in Brazilian Cultural Studies at the Helen Kellogg Institute for International Studies at the University of Notre Dame in 2006 and a John Simon Guggenheim Memorial Foundation fellow in 2008.

At our respective universities we have many to thank, including Nilda Flores González, Amalia Pallares, and Ralph Cintron, who participated at the University of Illinois at Chicago's conference on Engaged Youths and gave us critical feedback. Cathy Cohen, Jim Block, and Molly Andolina did as well. Irene Rizzini is grateful for the support for and recognition of her work from her colleagues at the Pontifical Catholic University of Rio de Janeiro. At the Universidad Autónoma Metropolitana, Luz María Chapela and Samuel Salinas presented the youths' publication.

We all worked with committed and amazing students: In Chicago, Dolores Muñoz, Phoebe Connolly, and Nawojka Lesinski; in Mexico City, Nathalie Coutu and Santiago Martínez Rubio. In Rio, we are grateful to the CIESPI research team, particularly Paula Caldeira, Marcelo Princeswal, Alessandra Caldeira, and Denise Barros. Professor Udi Mandel Butler from Bristol University has made an important contribution to this and other research projects.

Childwatch International gave us the opportunity to meet and discuss our project with colleagues throughout the Americas, especially Gloria Lopez and Yuherqui Guaimaro of CENDIF of the Universidad Metropolitana de Caracas and Graciela Tonon and her team of the Universidad de Lomas de Zamora, Argentina, who are applying our methodology to the study of activists in their respective countries.

Ileana Orozo worked her editorial magic on our multilingual, multidisciplinary writings. We are deeply appreciative of our colleagues at the University of Illinois Press, especially Joan Catapano, Larin McLaughlin, and Willis Regier, who believed in this project and shepherded it through various stages. To our reviewers we owe special thanks for their insightful suggestions.

We are most grateful to the activists who trusted us with their personal experiences.

Each of us is also deeply appreciative of the support that our husbands have given us through these years; Matthew Piers, Malcolm Bush, and Ignacio Durán. We also dedicate this book to them.

CITIZENS IN THE PRESENT

ONE

Civically Engaged Youth

Maria de los Angeles Torres, Irene Rizzini,
and Norma Del Río

In the Americas in the beginning of the twentieth century, some observers expected the emergence of independent nations in which citizens would participate in decisions that affected their lives. For many of these observers, one of the foundations of these democratic societies was the children, who would be trained to be active citizens and, eventually, would take leadership positions at various levels in their societies (Dewey 1916; Martí 1979; Rodo 1961; Mariátegui 1988). The idea of training children and young people to be future leaders had been a concern of philosophers for centuries (Plato 1941; Rousseau 1956; Locke 1979); however, this new, modern, rational project promised a historical transformation in which large numbers of citizens would be included in the deliberation and administration of public policies. Even so, the children's citizenship and leadership roles were to be in their futures, not in their present, while they were still children. Democratic theory did not contemplate a role for children in the public arena, since it was deemed that they were not yet capable of making rational, informed decisions (Kulynych 2001; Bennett 2003). Indeed, some observers vehemently opposed their participation on the grounds that children were to be nurtured and protected in the private sphere, not thrown into the chaos of the public (Bethke Elshtain 1995). Exceptions were made in times of war, when extraordinary circumstances placed extraordinary demands on both women and children (Tuttle 1993).

Despite this philosophical and institutional exclusion, young people have sought ways to have a meaningful voice in the public arena and have challenged the precepts that effectively excluded them from the public. Many societies have responded by lowering the voting age. In the United States and in Mexico, it was lowered from twenty-one to eighteen following the widespread student mobilizations that took place in 1968. Perhaps the most emblematic action has been the United Nations' passage, in 1989, of the Convention on the Rights of the Child, which includes their right to have a voice in decisions that affect their lives. Subsequently there has been a flurry of governmental and nongovernmental organization (NGO) attention to creating institutions and practices that give children and young people a voice. Additionally, countless projects have debated and prescribed the best ways to instill a sense of civic responsibility in children and young people (Flanagan and Sherrod 1998; Haste and Torney-Purta 1992).

Still, as we started this research project, young people were predominantly viewed as apathetic and uninterested in politics. In the United States, for example, one particularly gloomy forecast cautioned that the future of democracy was in peril given the overall decline in participation (Putnam 2001). This was alarming. But a decline in *traditional* modes of political participation may not mean an overall decline, since engagement and, indeed, values attached to why and how citizens engage may vary from culture to culture, even within nations, and from generation to generation (Vinken 2005). This has certainly been the case in Latin America, which has witnessed a tidal wave of democratizing activities and the rise of countless grassroots and community-based organizations active in a variety of fields (Escobar and Álvarez 1992). There have also been visible signs of increased youth involvement throughout the world (Welton and Wolf 2001). And after 2006, when young people took to the streets in the largest marches in its history demanding immigration reform, scholars saw the beginning of a generational change (Pallares and Flores-Gonzalez 2010). They also noted increases in traditional forms of participation as young people turned out in record numbers for presidential elections in many countries in the Americas (Youniss and Levine 2009).

In our three cities—Chicago, Rio de Janeiro, and Mexico City—we knew of young people who cared deeply about their communities and were actively engaged in a variety of public issues. Still, we knew very little about these activists, their concerns or *inquietudes,* their trajectories, their political and social practices, and their ideas. Who were these young people? How did they become involved? How do they engage? What are their political ideas?

1. Young Brazilian activists. Photo by Manuelle Rosa.

Were there lessons to be learned from their engagement that could inform policies aimed at increasing the civic engagement of other young people? What could their actions tell us about democratic practices in cities in the Americas today? These are the central questions we posed to the young activists in our three cities.

Broader Context

The Changing Place of Youth in Public Discourses

We started our research by trying to understand the broad political context in which youth engagement was unfolding, including the place of youth in contemporary public discourses. We noted that young people did not hold the magical place in political discourses they had in the past. In all three countries studied, youth had been central to nation building in the past century. Compulsory public education, which included lessons on how to become a good citizen, had been expanded to all children and young people. Special projects, albeit with mixed results, were put in place to bring children and young people from the margins—among them orphans, Native Americans, and refugees from communism—into the national project (Rizzini 2002; Holt 1992; Adams 1995; Torres 2004).

By the mid-twentieth century, young people in the Americas were entering the political stage not as passive model citizens but rather as activists. The postwar boom had not resulted in egalitarianism. The Cold War had engendered military and authoritarian regimes throughout the Americas, supported by the United States, which had itself been involved in an unpopular war in Vietnam and was undergoing internal social upheavals. New social movements emerged in which young people were critical of governments. They were fueled by what the Brazilian anthropologist Alzira de Abreu in 2000 described as engagement born of feelings of constant impatience with injustice, with the anger that comes from arbitrary power, and with the association of intolerance with complicity and culpability.

Youth became the target of repressive forces seeking to reestablish order. In 1964, a United States–backed military regime came to power in Brazil, instituting a series of repressive measures, many aimed at young people in university settings. In 1968, young people took to the streets in Mexico City, only to be met by repressive government forces. On October 2, days before the opening of the Olympic Games, more than five hundred young people were killed by government forces as they protested repression and demanded a more egalitarian society. Also in 1968, Chicago's mayor ordered the police to shoot to kill if necessary to subdue the young protesters who had gathered during the Democratic National Convention.

Youth as agents of change, then, came to hold a special place in the 1960s. They were especially influenced by Jean-Paul Sartre's notion of engagement as a personal commitment to a project, or *proyecto de vida* (Sartre 1960), and by socialist promises of world equality and peace. Youth activists were both acting on and forging a social narrative that viewed young people as motors of change (Luzzatto 1997) and assumed that engagement was part of becoming a social being. Youth had disrupted the prescriptive developmental model that saw children as the citizens of the future. They had become rebels with an anti-establishment cause.

As youth became a *political* social category symbolizing change, this created anxieties. In the past twenty-five years, the place of young people in society and our concerns about them have continued to undergo drastic changes (Tyyska 2005). Children and youth—particularly those who are members of socially marginalized communities—have become objects of social derision (Grossberg 2001). Indeed, many have become objects of fear (Giroux 2003)—specifically, Latinos and African Americans in the United

States, indigenous groups and the poor in Mexico, and Afro-Brazilians in Brazil, especially the "street children."

Social fears have resulted in changes to the social and legal mechanisms that had been put in place to educate and protect young people. In many countries, public education is no longer seen as central to the future of the nation. Young people are unevenly protected in the criminal justice system. In the United States, a minor convicted of the same crime as an adult serves a longer jail sentence. And increasingly, Congress has eroded juvenile rights (Arteaga 2002). In all three countries studied, both violence against young people and violence carried out by them are increasing at alarming rates (Reguillo Cruz 2004). Young people of color are more vulnerable in Brazil and the United States, as are the poor in all three cities.

Paradoxically, as youth are feared, they are nonetheless given currency in a consumer market that both appeals to them and uses them to appeal to others (Maira and Soep 2005). Some scholars have argued that the concept of "youth" has been repackaged as a consumer category to serve the needs of global markets. Yet this artificial notion of a homogeneous "youth" can hide the deep differences in which young people of various backgrounds experience being young.

Young people, then, are commonly seen as consumers and in some cases as criminals, but their role as social activists is generally not recognized. This presents a special disjuncture, particularly given the current, dramatic demographic shift, in which young people make up an increasing percentage of the population in urban areas throughout the world.

Changing Public Spaces

The nature of the public spaces in which young people engage has also changed (Held 1999). Theoretically, democracies were conceived as political systems that relied on citizen input in the forms of electing representatives and participating in some fashion in the deliberations of public policy. The vote was a right given to "capable adults," a definition that often excluded women, individuals who did not own property or were not literate, and children and young people. In the last century, more countries—including those subjected to military regimes like Brazil or single party authoritarian governments like Mexico—opted for systems that had some form of citizen participation. Slowly, the definition of who was entitled to participate expanded, and younger members were included. In Brazil, the vote is compulsory for everyone over eighteen and voluntary for those aged sixteen to eighteen. As mentioned above, in Mexico and the United States, voting begins at eighteen.

As children's rights, including political rights, have become an intense focus of worldwide attention, many countries have responded by creating special councils that give young people a political platform in which to deliberate policies that affect them. Brazil codified into national law the United Nations Convention on the Rights of the Child and has a series of regional and municipal children's and youth's rights councils that monitor compliance with the law; these councils have various degrees of effectiveness but still recognize the importance of young people's voices. In addition, councils at the municipal, state, and federal level make an effort to include young people in the process of deliberation of policies that affect them. Mexico issued the Law for the Protection of the Rights of Children and Adolescents in 2000.

But even as young people were gaining acceptance in political systems, the last decades of the twentieth century brought forth new challenges that compromised the promise of more egalitarian and participatory societies, particularly for individuals without formal ties, or with weak ties, to the institutions of decision making. Globalization and neoliberal policies aimed at expanding its markets accelerated the bifurcation of economies, which created wider schisms between those who have access to the people and institutions that make public decisions and those who do not. Even political scientists who have followed democratization trends in the Americas by focusing on formal arrangements for public participation admit that democracies perhaps can be sustained only in settings where a rich social and economic fabric provides some level of egalitarianism (O'Donnell 2001). They ask: Can political democracies be sustained in societies marked by profound economic inequalities (APSA 2004)? Some argue that citizenship can be conceived as a space of "condensation of accumulated disadvantages" at the same time as the site of possibility of agency as it is also a mediational category that defines the relationship of social subjects to the state and at the same time protects these same subjects from the power of the state (Reguillo Cruz 2005). This is a particularly urgent question for young people who seek a voice in their political communities, since they do not have an institutionalized voice, and they are disproportionately affected by poverty and vulnerable to state abuses.

Democracies were also conceived as residing within specific nation-states where some form of legal system set up participatory procedures and defined the rights of citizens. Yet recent economic and cultural changes across the world have affected the structure of politics and identity, as well as the spaces in which youth can engage (Cannella and Kincheloe 2002; Kaufman Hevener and Rizzini 2002). Globalization challenges the boundaries of nation-states but does not necessarily provide protections beyond them. The nation-state is no longer the exclusive organizer of our economies, politics, or selves, especially for immigrants and their children, whose lives span multiple states. This brings forth the question of what entity would guarantee rights that could be violated by multiple states and transnational entities (Bauman 1998). Indeed, after the September 11, 2001, terrorist attack in the United States, especially designated areas, such as Guantanamo Base in Cuba, have been exempt from any international or national rights protection. Some scholars have proposed that cities would become the critical links in a new global economy and consequently that cities would become the spaces in which meaningful politics could be played out (Sassen 1991). But cities themselves are deeply divided along a multiplicity of lines, and they, too, function within a larger set of societal rules and structures just as they respond to the exigencies of global capital.

These profound economic and political changes raised questions about politics in general and specifically about the nature of public engagement (Klymlicka 1999). At the same time that large systemic changes could be limiting access to policy making, they could also be creating new public spaces in which young activists might forge new practices (Driskell, Fox, and Kudva 2008).

Our Study

Studying Youth Engagement: Receptors or Protagonists?

An important part of our comparative research process was developing an understanding of the ways in which youth engagement has been studied. This included reading studies done in our individual countries as well as looking at the more contemporary global literature of youth engagement.

In the United States, political socialization studies were in vogue in the late 1960s, when great youth movements worldwide were demanding radical changes, and notions about the place of children and their care were changing (Block 2002). Social scientists began asking how children and youth acquired their political ideas and habits (Sapiro 2004). They found that children do have a political life that in part begins with a sense of place, usually the nation, and includes feelings about authority figures and knowledge about political processes and issues (Greenstein 1965; Hess and Torney 1968; Easton and Dennis 1969; Sigel 1969). Children's political development was initially studied following Piaget's stages of development

(Piaget 1932). There seemed to be certain stages of development in political attitudes, although these varied for young people of different backgrounds and nationalities (Jahoda 1963). A variety of socializing agents, from parents to teachers to peers, influence children's political behavior (Jennings and Niemi 1974). Class differences can change the ways in which political socialization unfolds (Hirsch 1971). And some traditions also mattered (Connell 1971; Jennings and Niemi 1981). Other scholars have looked at the role of political knowledge and how this may affect political behavior. Some found that race, class, and educational attainment had an impact on political knowledge (Delli Carpini and Keeter 1997).

The emphasis of these studies was on how young people became socialized into an existing political order, not how they acted on it, much less how they tried to change it. Recently, there are those who have urged a more transgressive view of youth activism. Community psychologists, for instance, have insisted that social justice and change-oriented activism should be studied alongside more traditional forms of activism (Prilleltensky and Fox 2007; Watts and Flanagan 2007). And political scientists have again turned their eyes toward youth political engagement (Niemi and Hepburn 1995).

In Mexico, political socialization literature followed the same path. A classic study found that children and young people inherited authoritarian views of politics through the family structure (Segovia 1977). Other studies sought to document political knowledge and found low levels of political information (González Navarro and Garduño 2006; Nateras Domínguez 2007; Reimers 2008; Tirado Segura and Guevara Niebla 2006). Others studied the trajectories of politicians and found that the higher the level the politician reached, the more family involvement in training their children there had been, thus suggesting a close interconnected network of family values and interests in the promotion of their children into political offices (López Lara and Loza Otero 2003; Camp 1986, 1996, 44; Ruiz Sánchez 2008).

In Brazil, political socialization studies came later—they emerged after the fall of the military dictatorship in the early 1980s—and were focused on understanding youth engagement. Brazilian writers have demonstrated that contemporary young people are engaged in a variety of ways, and these writers have questioned the idea that, in general, young people are indifferent or apathetic (Abramo and Branco 2005; Castro and Correa 2005; Novaes and Vital 2002; Abramovay and Castro 2006; Rizzini, Pereira, and Thapliyal 2007; Silva 2007). Major changes in young people's participation in traditional political organizations are, according to some authors, linked to changes in political discourse and practice that have made it easier for young people to become involved in the public sphere and in discussions about social issues (Butler, Princeswal and Abreu 2007).

Another important feature of the Brazilian literature on youth engagement is found in a series of studies completed in the past several years that used participatory methodologies to sketch out the opinions of young people on a variety of topics. These studies include surveys by a variety of national organizations such as the Institute for Religious Studies (ISER 2002), the Brazilian Institute for Social and Economic Analyses (IBASE 2005), the Institute for Studies, Training, and the Consultancy in Social Policies (IBASE and Instituto Pólis 2005), as well as international institutions such as the United Nations Organization for Education, Science, and Culture (Abramovay and García 2006) and the United Nations Children's Fund (UNICEF 2007). These surveys included questions that permitted analyses of the general patterns of youth's civic participation in several Brazilian metropolitan regions, as well as on the political, social, and religious aspects of the civic involvement of young people.

Most of the political socialization studies, even the later ones, were conducted at a time when the modernist paradigm influenced the definition and the operation of politics and childhood. Politics was organized primarily within the borders of nation-states, and it had meaning in the lives of many people, including those of children. In *The Political Life of Children* (2000), for instance, Robert Coles related how a few dozen children from seven countries constructed their political world. What he found from the children he interviewed was that their political lives were influenced by national political cultures. Other studies also noted cultural differences in different political and philosophical traditions embraced by young people (Claussen and Mueller 1990).

We turned to studies that followed youth in action in situations where they could be influenced by national and global cultures. Globally there has been an increasing interest in children and young people as political protagonists, and important work has documented activist youths (Sherrod et al. 2005; Sigel 1995; Sapiro 2004; Ardizzone 2007). Scholars have also analyzed projects to see to what extent young people participated in decision making and planning of these organizations (Cahill and Hart 2006; Hart 1992). The literature demonstrates, then, that young people may absorb a body of knowledge and a set of practices, but they may also act as protagonists. Our study explores both how they acquire knowledge and interest and how and why they act.

Defining the Terms

Youth

As we started to think about whom we would interview and what questions we would pose, we found that we needed to clarify two concepts: youth and civic engagement. We realized that we brought different disciplinary perspectives to our understanding of young people (Alpízar and Bernal 2003), and that we had different national viewpoints as well.

Notions of age-related categories are malleable, change throughout time, and unfold in particular social settings (Aries 1962; Erikson 1963). Children and young people also have different national experiences (Fass and Mason 2000). Historically, changes in technology have radically altered the ways that information is presented and distributed, and consequently have changed the boundaries of childhood (Postman 1994). Indeed, our own concept of youth may be symptomatic of these structural changes, as there may be a globally driven construction of a youth culture (Feixa 1999).

Our conceptions of youth are also affected by social and economic realities that vary across countries (James and James 2004). The studies on youth in Latin America insist that there are many realities of childhood and youth (Dávila León 2004; Reguillo Cruz and Feixa 2005). Scholars of urban youth in the United States have provided similar perspectives on how gender, race, and ethnicity create different experiences in similar age groups (Tienda and Wilson 2002). These differences cut across all aspects of life including health, education, and interactions with law enforcement.

But even taking into account these differences, there may be integrated youth experiences that help establish a sense of a social group even as they experience living it in a variety of ways. There may be developmental experiences as well that contribute to a sense of identity and social activism (Erikson 1968).

In 2004, the Economic Commission for Latin America (CEPAL) enumerated a series of contradictions that mark youth in Latin America that may be applicable to their counterparts in the United States. These include more access to education, but less employment; more information, but less power; a higher expectation of autonomy, but few means to achieve it. Politically, young people are being affected by policies and expect to be protagonists of change, but they are not always aware of how to influence these choices.

There are qualitative aspects to the notion of youth that have an impact on how we define it. A 2003 United Nations World Youth Report defines the phase we call youth as a time when a person moves from dependence

2. La Fuerza Juventud. Photo by Amalia Pallares.

(childhood) to independence (adulthood) and identifies four distinct aspects of this transition:

- Leaving the parental home and establishing new living arrangements;
- Completing full-time education;
- Forming close, stable personal relationships outside of the family, often resulting in marriage and children; and
- Testing the labor market, finding work and possibly settling into a career, and achieving a more or less sustainable livelihood.

These measures are deeply affected by economic restructuring that has been brought about by globalization (Katz 2004). More youth are living at home, and even after completing their education, many are not finding viable employment and are postponing marriage and parenthood. These developments were more visible in Rio and Mexico City, although they were becoming more common for young people in Chicago, as well. The ages included in the definition of *youth* are also simultaneously being pushed downward as the boundaries that contained childhood have eroded (Nilan and Feixa 2006) and upward as life spans lengthen.

In quantitative terms, youths are commonly defined as people between the ages of fifteen and twenty-four. That definition is used by both the United Nations and the World Bank and in many institutional statistics and indicators. But in the United States, *youth* is usually understood to end a little sooner, although this is changing. In Brazil, the category has slowly extended to include those in their late twenties. While understanding the differences in definition, we started by interviewing young people from fifteen to twenty-four and left the door open to include younger and older individuals in the study.

Civic Engagement

Once we reached an understating of our definition of *youth*, we needed to agree on whom we would be approaching. How would we define *engagement*? What organizations would we include in our study? This turned out to be a complicated discussion, since *engagement* raises conceptual and practical issues. What does it mean to the individual? What is its place in each of our societies? How is the term *political* understood? What are the locations of engagement? What should the length of engagement be?

The Civic

According to the historian Antoine Prost (1998), *civic engagement* is a phenomenon that emerged in its present form in the twentieth century, once longstanding obstacles to freedom of association and expression diminished. In that century, unions, political parties, reform movements, and civic associations grew in the public sphere. These processes played out differently within national cultures, and indeed we had national contrasts in our understanding of the concept of civic engagement. In the United States, the term *civic engagement* connotes a positive set of actions that have long been recognized as one of the hallmarks of its political system (de Tocqueville 2003). It has been generally assumed that for democracies to work, citizens need to be engaged in a series of informal civic networks through which trust develops (Almond and Verba 1965). For others, like Hannah Arendt (1998), an active life is a prerequisite for an individual living in a plurality, and its purpose was to actualize our capacity for freedom.

In contrast, in Mexico, decades of corrupt and paternalistic politics have discouraged people, the young in particular, from becoming involved in politics (Monsiváis Carillo 2004). Young people are especially disillusioned with political parties (Cuna Perez 2006; Cuna Perez, Perez, and Laura 2006). In Brazil, the term *civic* came to be associated with the sanctioned form of being a loyal citizen to the military regime and is often contrasted with *citizenship*, a notion that connotes a series of rights, not just responsibilities.

Civic or Political?

Civic activities are often distinguished from political actions. From this perspective, *civic* includes everything originating from citizens or nongovernmental organizations, and *political* describes actions involved with the state, usually through state-linked organizations (Locke 1955). In democracies, the most important political activity is the vote. It is such a necessary feature in emerging democracies that it, along with other electoral activities, is emphasized by those studying citizen participation in politics. Voting studies have been especially rich in countries in which the right to vote has been extended to new groups. For many democracies, voting became an arena of intense struggle as excluded groups—the young, in some cases—fought for their rights. Voting became a window through which broad societal engagement could be examined.

More recently, some scholars studying the activism of young people have suggested operational distinctions between civic and political activities and

3. Mikva Challenge students and Senator Richard Durbin. Photo by Mikva Challenge.

have categorized activities as civic, electoral, and political. *Civic* in this definition pertains more to volunteer and charitable work; *electoral* is tied to promoting a candidate or a party, and *political* is aimed at having an influence on the political system (Keeter et al. 2002; Zukin et al. 2006). These studies sought to expand the notion of the political beyond voting, a narrow definition that would be a limitation in studying young people, since voting is generally restricted to those over a certain age.

This distinction may still exclude important forms of public action. Even as youths are kept out of public political spaces (Lesinski 2008), the boundaries between public and private institutions are porous, and it is almost impossible to conceive of equality in one realm but not the other. To achieve equality, both public and private spheres need to be transformed. Furthermore, the institutions that provide access to power or, for that matter, that exercise power are not only governmental—they can be educational, financial, or media related. Power itself is diffuse, and its institutionalization and its contestation are heavily influenced by ideas and images found in the media. Particularly young people are aware of this dimension (Barnhurst 1998). Collective action aimed at influencing public decisions can take on many forms, and it can have many targets.

One useful definition of *civic engagement* is the following:

> individual and collective actions designed to identify and address issues of public concern. Civic engagement can take many forms, from individual volunteerism to organizational involvement to electoral participation. It can include efforts to directly address an issue, work with others in a community to solve a problem or interact with the institutions of representative democracy. (Delli Carpini 2010)

We began to think of how civic and social action could have explicit political meaning, keeping in mind that political action also contributes to developing a civic culture and a sense of community. We felt it was important to include actions aimed at influencing decisions at a variety of private and public institutions. We chose to define *political and civic activities* more broadly in order to capture what may be nontraditional forms of engagement, which may be particularly significant in appreciating youthful activism (Novaes and Vital 2006; Aduriz and Ava 2006; C. Cohen 2005). In that way, we agreed with contemporary democratic theorists who argue for a broader vision of what the political encompasses (Pateman 1976; J. Cohen and Arato 1994).

The Spaces of Engagement

But how broad? Would these spaces include cultural organizations? What about actions aimed at educational institutions and the media? Have recent technologies created new spaces for engagement? We decided to look at a broad range of activities as long as they were aimed at changing or influencing ideas, situations, institutions, and decisions that affected the youths.

We were also interested in the geographic dimensions of space and politics (Skelton 2010). Traditionally, the nation-state has been one of the most important units for understanding political engagement. Did this still hold in a globalized world? Had globalization expanded the geographies of political communities as it had those of youth cultures (Skelton and Valentine 1998)? Where did young people locate themselves in the global, the national, the local?

We were also open to including virtual spaces. Did young activists use and engage new technologies to create their political communities?

Social and Political Identities and Engagement

Spaces are not just geographically or technologically created; they also consist of a social fabric. What are the communities from which young people speak? What are the communities they are forging in the process of speaking and acting collectively? Notions of racial and ethnic identities and indeed national ones—so integral to the political process—are in flux. More young people, for example, now embrace multiple identities even though in some societies they are reclaiming single religious and racially informed identities. Many reject imperial national identities like "American." Class continues to be a defining category, even as it is embedded in residential communities or in racial and ethnic categories. How do young people define these social communities? Is age one indicator? If so, what are the features of age as a political category at this historical juncture?

Underpinning the theory of collective political action is also the notion of citizenship, the concept of rights held by the individual. An important step for us was appreciating that citizenship is not a static concept, and that new forms of citizenship could be emerging in broad social movements (Dagnino 2004). Some scholars have proposed a notion of cultural citizenship, a citizenship that not only endows narrow legal rights but that also takes into account social and political identities (Flores and Benmayor 1998). Still, it entails expectations about rights and responsibilities, and we asked our participants about their notions of those. We also considered ideas about the relationship of citizens to the state and about the responsibilities the state has to citizens. How do young activists situate themselves individually and as a social group in the state, and how do they interact with its decision-making apparatuses?

Temporalities of Engagement

Finally, we asked: If children and youth have been considered citizens of the future and not the present, where do young activists situate themselves? The discussion about time is important because time affects the location of the individual in political projects. Are young people given rights in the present, or are they only conceived as future citizens?

Time also affects the scale of political projects. Essential to modernity was the idea of progress in stages. Our discussion of temporalities brought us into debates about modernity and postmodernity, particularly as it related to Latin America (Munck 2000; Quijano 1993). Do the notions of modernity and perhaps postmodernity reflect universal values, or are they specific to imperial notions of history (de Sousa Santos 1995)? Postmodernity posits a certain set of assumptions about a previous stage, modernity, that includes the existence of independent nation-states with democratic governments. Some countries that were dependent on colonial powers never reached this kind of independence, and their governments more often than not were authoritarian. It could be argued that colonial powers were not independent either. In thinking through these dilemmas in regard to young people, one author asks, how can young people be postmodern if they have never been modern (Castillo Berthier 2008)? Specifically, how do people who grow up in a postcolonial society that is not democratic internalize truly democratic principles? Furthermore, human societies may evolve within simultaneous temporalities. In fact, the coexistence of multiple temporalities may be part of the essence of Latin American reality as "modern" and "traditional" temporalities easily co-exist (Calderón 1993; Ramos Lara 2007).

Despite these limitations, there were important ideas generated from our discussions about modernity and postmodernity that helped us reach an understanding of how we could appreciate the narrative of young people about their political projects and ideas. Postmodern theorists question the ability of large transformative projects to change the world. This notion opens the door to understanding that political projects may be small and modest in scale, located in local and neighborhood politics. Is a postmodern world one in which the more porous boundaries of nation-states in some ways make possible universal categories of identity, or do they further fragment identities? How did young people identify themselves? How do they think about their political projects? Perhaps there were no grand ideological frameworks guiding young activists' political actions as there had been in the 1960s. The reorganization of power also leaves open the possibilities for new forms of political activism (Handler 1992). Postmodernity has put in doubt the temporality of modernity, particularly its futuristic predictions along paths of development or stages of growth that is the essence of the predictive model that children can be conceived as future citizens.

Location

Three Global Cities

We were interested in locating our study in global cities, since most youth live in urban areas, and since cities play such an important role in global restructuring. We chose Mexico City, Rio de Janeiro, and Chicago because high percentages of their populations are people fifteen to twenty-nine years old. These cities have distinct social, cultural, and political entities, but they share a hemispheric set of historical experiences. While the scales of the poverty

are different, all three cities are marked by deep structural inequalities that
take on distinct forms that deeply affect their young people (Tompkins and
Sternberg 2004). In Latin America, one in three young people live in poverty
(CEPAL 2004). Rio is characterized by systematic poverty that includes class
and racial dimensions as well as those of age. Mexico City, the largest of the
three cities, has historical divides between the rich and poor as geographic
location becomes a signifier of class and access. More than half of its population live in poverty, while 10 percent control almost half of the country's
wealth. Chicago is one of the most racially segregated cities in the world,
one in which national origin, immigration status, and race mark geographic
communities in distinct ways.

Violence is a common occurrence in the life of many young people, especially those who live in poverty. In Brazil, mortality rates for young males
are extraordinarily high and have increased in the past twenty years; the rates
are ten times higher than those for young women. A report sponsored by the
Brazilian government to mark the twentieth anniversary of the passage of the
pathbreaking Statute on the Child and the Adolescent notes an increase in
the murder rate of young people twelve to eighteen years old in Brazil, from
18.7 per 100,000 in 1997 to 24.1 per 100,000 in 2007 (Rizzini 2010).

4. Protest play in Rio de Janeiro. Photo by Manuelle Rosa.

In Mexico City, males are twice as likely to be victims of violence as females (INEGI, 2007). The homicide rate in 2008 rose to almost 12 per 100,000 inhabitants, which surpasses the threshold of 10 per 100,000 set by the World Health Organization to consider it as "epidemic" (Geremía 2011).

These cities have become arenas of intense political and social struggles around issues that directly affect the young people living, studying, and working in them (Tranberg Hansen 2008; Castells 1985). They are also stages on which national events unfold. In all three cities, young people have played important roles in key national political events. Chicago is home to Barack Obama, who was first elected to the state senate in 1996, rose to the U.S. Senate in 2006, and in 2008 became the first African American president of the United States. Young people played key a part in his campaign, leading to a generational change in electoral politics not seen in the past fifty years. In Rio, Luis Ignacio "Lula" da Silva, the head of the most significant progressive party in Brazil, Partido dos Trabalhadores, the Workers Party (PT), was elected president in 2002 after three previous unsuccessful attempts at that office, signaling a shift in national politics in favor of workers and the poor (Rizzini and Barker 2002). And in 2000, Mexico's electorate ended the rule of the Partido Revolucionario Institucional (PRI), a political party that had been in power since the Mexican Revolution of 1917. All three cities have been part of the political drama that has contributed to these changes and has marked a generation of young people. We felt that as distinct as these cities were, their political histories and contemporary struggles made it reasonable to investigate the activism of their youth. We were keenly aware that the differences in each city framed the ways in which young people were defined and engaged in political actions.

Methodology

Our goal was to talk to young activists. Unlike most of the literature on youth and activism, which looks at problems (Helve and Holm 2005), we were interested in understanding youth who were involved in their societies. We sought out organizations with projects that facilitated the empowerment of young people, were rooted in communities, and responded to grassroots agendas. Because many of these organizations are involved in reclaiming rights and improving the quality of life for the less affluent communities, they tend to be on the progressive spectrum of politics and they attract young people who share their political orientation (this was not meant to exclude organizations with more conservative leanings). Still these were not ideological organizations or for that matter political parties with a preconceived platform of ideas.

We did aim to have a diverse group of organizations involved in a variety of activities to understand engagement in its broadest possible meaning as well as to include diversity in forms of engagement.

See the appendix for a list of participants, organizations, and activities.

We tried to balance racial and ethnic identities in Chicago, as these are critical to the ways people identify themselves in the United States. Geographic diversity was also important, since these cities are made up of many distinct zones and geographically dispersed communities. Again, because of the nature of the organizations, the majority of participants could be classified as working class, although several participants in each city could be classified as children of middle-class professionals.

Meetings with young organizers from a variety of groups helped us identify activists who were willing to be part of this project. We asked them to help us recruit the most active leaders in their organizations. It was our intention to seek out those who were articulate about their activism. We were not looking for a random sample, but rather an intentionally constructed sample of leader/activists. After the individuals were identified, we had initial meetings with them, and when necessary we contacted their parents to ask for their consent.

We attended many of the organizations' events, including film screenings, poetry slams, political discussions, meetings, and retreats. At the end of the first phase, twenty-five young people consented to participate in Chicago, twenty-four in Rio, and twenty-two in Mexico City.

We wanted to bring first-person narratives into the study of youth politics. The interviews we conducted were transcribed. The participants were asked to read the transcripts and add any information that they wanted to share. We also asked them to write essays about their ideas. We had several workshops in which they were asked to present the essays and give one another feedback. The idea was to provide an opportunity for them to develop their narratives and share them with other youth activists throughout their city. The participants who wrote the essays decided they would like to publish them, and they organized events in each of the cities to launch their publications. Community organizers, teachers, parents, and relatives were invited to attend. For our book, we asked the participants if they wanted us to use their names or pseudonyms. Participants in Chicago wanted to use their names in the essays and in our writings. For participants in Rio de Janeiro and Mexico City, pseudonyms are used in this book.

The initial interviews in all three cities followed similar formats. The young people were asked about their personal backgrounds and their political histories, the issues important to them, their activities, their ideas about authority, rights, and responsibilities, their political beliefs and their perceptions of their place in the world.

This book relies on the interviews we conducted in each of the three cities. While we were tempted to present the material along thematic lines, in the end we chose to present it by city. We followed similar themes in each chapter: becoming involved, engaging, and envisioning. We believe the ideas of young activists in these three global cities can deepen our understanding of democratic practices in the world today. In the final chapter, we come back to the conceptual questions raised in this introduction, and since this is a qualitative study, we suggest avenues that other researchers may want to pursue.

References

Abramo, H., and P. Branco eds. 2005. *Retratos da Juventude Brasileira: Análises de uma pesquisa nacional.* São Paulo: Fundação Perseu Abramo/Instituto Cidadania.

Abramovay, Miriam, and Mary Garcia Castro, eds. 2006. *Juventude, Juventudes: O que une e o que separa.* Brasília: UNESCO. Retrieved from http://www.unesco .org.br/publicacoes/livros/juventudesjuventude/mostra_documento.

Abreu, Alzira Alves de. 2000. "A Imprensa e o engajamento político no final do século XX." 24 Encontro Anual da ANPOCS. Petrópolis. Retrieved from http:// bibliotecavirtual.clacso.org.ar/ar/libros/anpocs00/gt08/00gt0813.doc.

Adams, David Wallace. 1995. *Education for Extinction: American Indians and the Boarding School Experience, 1875–1928.* Kansas: University of Kansas Press.

Aduriz, Isidro, and Pablo Ava. 2006. "Construcción de Ciudadanía: Experiencia de Implementación de un Índice de Participación Ciudadana en América Latina." *América Latina de Hoy* 42: 15–35.

Almond, Gabriel, and Sidney Verba. 1965. *The Civic Culture: Political Attitudes and Democracy in Five Nations.* Boston: Little, Brown.

Alpízar, Lydia, and Marina Bernal. 2003. "La construcción social de las juventudes: Ultima Década." *Revista de el Centro de Investigación y Difusión de Población de Achupallas, Viña del Mar, Chile,* no. 019: 1–20. Retrieved from http://fundacion desafios.net/wp-content/uploads/descargas/Biblioteca/Construccion%20social %20de%20las%20juventudes.pdf.

APSA (American Political Science Association). 2004. Report of the Task Force on Inequality and American Democracy. *Political Science and Politics* 37, no. 3: 525. Retrieved from www.apsanet.org/content_2471.cfm.

Ardizzone, Leonisa. 2007. *Getting My Word Out: Voices of Urban Youth Activists.* New York: SUNY Press.

Arendt, Hannah. 1998. *The Human Condition.* 2nd ed. Chicago: University of Chicago Press.

Aries, Philip. 1962. *Centuries of Childhood: A Social History of Family Life.* Translated by Robert Baldick. New York: Vintage Books.

Arteaga, Juan Alberto. 2002. "Juvenile in Justice: Congressional Attempts to Abrogate the Procedural Rights of Juvenile Defendants. *Columbia Law Review* 102, no. 4: 1051–88.

Barnhurst, Kevin G. 1998. "Politics in the Fine Meshes: Young Citizens, Power and Media." *Media, Culture and Society* 20, no. 2: 201–18. Retrieved from http://mcs.sagepub.com/content/20/2/201.

Bauman, Zygmunt. 1998. *Globalization: The Human Consequences.* New York: Columbia University Press.

Bennett, Robert. 2003. *Talking It Through: Puzzles of American Democracy.* Ithaca, NY: Cornell University Press.

Bethke Elshtain, Jean. 1995. "Political Children." In *Feminist Interpretations of Hannah Arendt*, edited by Bonni Honig, 263–84. University Park: Pennsylvania State University Press.

Block, James. 2002. *A Nation of Agents: The American Path to a Modern Self and Society.* Cambridge, MA: Harvard University Press.

Butler, U., M. Princeswal, and R. Abreu. 2007. *Relatório de pesquisa do projeto Culturas de Participação: Jovens e suas práticas de cidadania.* CIESPI. Retrieved from http://www.ciespi.org.br.

Cahill, Caitlin, and Roger A. Hart. 2006. "Pushing the Boundaries: Critical International Perspectives on Child and Youth Participation Series." *Children, Youth and Environments* 16, no. 2.

Calderón, Fernando. 1993. "Latin American Identity and Mixed Temporalities: Or, How to Be Postmodern and Indian at the Same Time." *Boundary* 20, no. 3: 55–64.

Camp, Roderic. 1986. "Relaciones familiares en la política mexicana." *Foro Internacional* 26, no. 3 (enero–marzo): 349–72.

———. 1996. *Reclutamiento político en México, 1884–1991.* Mexico: Siglo XXI Editores.

Cannella, Gaile S., and Joe Kincheloe, eds. 2002. *Kidworld: Childhood Studies, Global Perspectives, and Education.* New York: Peter Lang.

Castells, Manuel. 1985. *The City and the Grassroots: A Cross-Cultural Theory of Urban Social Movements.* California Series in Urban Development. Berkeley: University of California Press.

Castillo Berthier, Héctor. 2008. "Juventud, cultura y política social: Un proyecto de investigación aplicada en la ciudad de México, 1987–2007." Mexico: IMJUVE-SEP.

Castro, L., and J. Correa, orgs. 2005. *Juventude contemporânea: Perspectivas nacionais e internacionais.* Coleção Infância e Adolescência no Contemporâneo. Rio de Janeiro: NAU Editora / FAPERJ.

CEPAL (Comisión Económica para América Latina y el Caribe). 2004. "La juventud en Iberoamérica Tendencias y Urgencias." Report no. LC/L2180. CEPAL-Instituto Iberoamericano de la Juventud.

Claussen, Hernhard, and Horst Mueller, eds. 1990. *Political Socialization of the Young in East and West.* Frankfurt am Main: Peter Lang.

Cohen, Cathy. 2006. "African American Youths: Broadening Our Understanding of Politics, Civic Engagement and Activism." *Youth Activism: A Web Forum Organized by the Social Science Research Council.* Retrieved from http://ya.ssrc.org/african/Cohen/.

Cohen, Jean L., and Andrew Arato. 1994. *Civil Society and Political Theory*. Cambridge, MA: MIT Press.

Coles, Robert. 2000. *The Political Life of Children*. New York: Atlantic Monthly Press.

Connell, R. W. 1971. *The Child's Construction of Politics*. Melbourne: Australia: Melbourne University Press.

Cuna Perez, Enrique. 2006. "Reflexiones sobre el desencanto democrático: El caso de los partidos políticos y los jóvenes en la ciudad de México." *Sociológica* 21: 95–134.

Dagnino, Evelina. 2004. "Sociedade civil, participacao e cidadania? De que estamos falando? In *Politicas de Ciudadania y sociedad civil en tiempos de globalizacion*, edited by Daniel Mato. Caracas: Faces, Universidad Central de Venezuela. 95–110.

Dávila León, Óscar. 2004. "Adolescencia y juventud: De las nociones a los abordajes." *Última Década* 2: 3–104.

Delli Carpini, Michael X. 2010. "Defining Civic Engagement." Alliance for Children and Families. Retrieved from http://alliance1.org/ce/defining-civic -engagement.

Delli Carpini, Michael X, and Scott Keeter. 1997. *What Americans Know about Politics and Why It Matters*. New Haven, CT: Yale University Press.

De Souza Santos, Boaventura. 1995. *Toward a New Common Sense: Law, Science, and Politics in the Paradigmatic Transition*. New York: Routledge.

de Tocqueville, Alexis. 2003. *Democracy in America*. London: Penguin Classics.

Dewey, John. 1916. *Democracy and Education: An Introduction to the Philosophy of Education*. New York: Macmillan.

Driskell, David, Carly Fox, and Neema Kudva. 2008. "Growing Up in the New New York: Youth Space, Citizenship and Community Change in a Hyperglobal City." *Environment and Planning* 40: 2831–44.

Easton, David, and Jack Dennis. 1969. *Children in the Political System*. New York: McGraw Hill.

Erikson, Eric. 1963. *Childhood and Society*. New York: W. W. Norton.

———. 1968. *Identity, Youth and Crisis*. New York: W. W. Norton.

Escobar, Arturo, and Sonia Álvarez, eds. 1992. *The Making of Social Movements In Latin America: Identity, Strategy, and Democracy*. Boulder, CO: Westview Press.

Fass, Paula S., and Mary Ann Mason, eds. 2000. *Childhood in America*. New York: New York University Press.

Feixa, Carles. 1999. *De Jóvenes, bandas y tribus: Antropología de la juventud*. Barcelona: Editorial Ariel.

Feixa, Carles. 2005. "The Socio-Cultural Construction of Youth in Latin America." In *Contemporary Youth Research: Local Expressions and Global Connections*, edited by Helena Helve and Gunilla Holm. Hants, UK: Ashgate.

Flanagan, Constance, and Lonnie Sherod. 1998. "Youth Political Development: An Introduction," *Journal of Social Issues* 54, no. 3 (Fall): 447–56.

Flores, William, and Rina Benmayor. 1998. *Latino Cultural Citizenship: Claiming Identity, Space, and Rights*. Boston: Beacon Press.

Geremía, V. 2011. "Infancia y conflicto armado en México." *Informe alternativo sobre el protocolo facultativo de la Convención sobre los Derechos del Niño relativo a la participación de niños en los conflictos armados*. Mexico: Red por los derechos de la Infancia en México-Infancia Cuenta-Fundación para la Protección de la Niñez IAP.

Giroux, Henry. 2003. *The Abandoned Generation: Democracy beyond the Culture of Fear*. New York: Palgrave Macmillan.

Greenstein, Fred. 1965. *Children and Politics*. New Haven, CT: Yale University Press.

González Navarro, Manuel, and Hyldely Garduño. 2006. "Cultura política en los jóvenes del Distrito Federal: Pensando la política." In *Representación social y cultura política en jóvenes mexicanos*, edited by Marco Antonio Gónzalez Pérez, 177–216. Mexico: Plaza y Valdés.

Grossberg, Lawrence. 2001. "Why Does Neo-Liberalism Hate Kids? The War on Youth and the Culture of Politics." *Review of Education/ Pedagogy/Cultural Studies* 23, no. 2: 111–36.

Handler, Joel. 1992. "Postmodernism, Protest, and the New Social Movements." *Law and Society Review* 26, no. 4: 697–732.

Hart, Roger A. 1992. "Children's Participation: From Tokenism to Citizenship. *Innonceti Essays*. No. 4. Florence, Italy: UNICEF International Child Development Centre.

Haste, Helen, and Judith Torney-Purta. 1992. *The Development of Political Understanding: A New Perspective*. San Francisco: Jossey-Bass.

Held, David. 1999. "The Transformation of Political Community." In *Democracy's Edges*, edited by Ian Shapiro and Casiano Hacker-Cordon. Cambridge: Cambridge University Press.

Helve, Helena, and Gunilla Holm, eds. 2005. *Youth Research: Local Expressions and Global Connections*. Aldershot: Ashgate.

Hess, Robert, and Judith Torney. 1968. *The Development of Political Attitudes in Children*. New York: Doubleday Anchor Books.

Hirsch, Herbert. 1971. *Poverty and Politicization: Political Socialization in an American Sub-Culture*. New York: Free Press.

Holt, Marilyn Irving. 2001. *The Orphan Trains: Placing Out in America*. Lincoln: University of Nebraska Press.

IBASE (Instituto Brasiliero de Análises Sociais e Econômicas). 2005. *Juventude Brasileira e democracia: Participação, esferas e políticas públicas*. Rio de Janeiro: IBASE.

IBASE and Instituto Pólis. 2005. *Juventude Brasileira e democracia: Participação, esferas e políticas públicas*. Rio de Janeiro: IBASE.

INEGI (Instituto Nacional de Estadística y Geografía). 2007. Estadísticas a propósito del día Internacional de la Juventud. Datos Nacionales. Retrieved from http://www.inegi.gob.mx/inegi/contenidos/espanol/prensa/contenidos/estadisticas/2007/jovenes07.pdf.

ISER (Instituto de Estudos da Religião). 1992. *Jovens do Rio: Circuitos, crenças e acessos*. Edited by Regina Novaes and Cecília Campello Mello. Rio de Janeiro: Comunicações do ISER.

Jahoda, Gustave. 1963. "The Development of Children's Ideas about Country and nationality." *British Psychological Society* 33, no. 1: 47–60.

James, Allison, and Adrian James. 2004. *Constructing Childhood: Theory, Policy and Social Practice*. New York: Palgrave Macmillan.

Jennings, Kent, and Richard Niemi. 1974. *The Political Character of Adolescents.* Princeton, NJ: Princeton University Press.

———. 1981. *Generations and Politics: A Panel Study of Young Adults and Their Parents.* Princeton, NJ: Princeton University Press.

Katz, Cindi. 2004. *Growing Up Global: Economic Restructuring and Children's Everyday Lives.* Minneapolis: University of Minnesota Press.

Kaufman Hevener, Natalie, and Irene Rizzini. 2002. *Globalization and Children: Exploring Potentials for Enhancing Opportunities in the Lives of Children and Youth.* New York: Kluwer Academic/Plenum.

Keeter, Scott, Cliff Zukin, Molly Andolina, and Krista Jenkins. 2002. *The Civic and Political Health of a Nation: A Generational Portrait.* Medford, MA: Center for Information and Research on Civic Learning and Engagement (CIRCLE).

Klymlicka, Will. 1999. "Citizenship in the Era of Globalization: A Comment on Held." In *Democracy's Edges,* edited by Ian Shapiro and Casiano Hacker-Cordon. Cambridge: Cambridge University Press.

Kulynych, Jessica. 2001. "No Playing in the Public Sphere: Democratic Theory and the Exclusion of Children." *Social Theory and Practice* 27, no. 2: 231–64.

Lesinski, Nawojka. 2008. "The Public Sphere: Checking ID at the Door?" Paper presented at the MPSA Annual National Conference, Palmer House Hilton Hotel, Chicago. Retrieved from http://www.allacademic.com/meta/p267290_index.html.

Locke, John. 1955. *Of Civil Government.* Chicago: Henry Regnery.

———. 1979. *An Essay Concerning Human Understanding.* Oxford: Oxford University Press.

López Lara, Álvaro, and Nicolás Loza Otero. 2003. "Viejos actores, nuevo poder: Los diputados locales en México." *Polis: Investigación y Análisis Sociopolítico y Psicosocial* 1, no. 3: 49–84.

Luzzatto, Sergio. 1997. "Young Rebels and Revolutionaries, 1789–1917." In *A History of Young People,* vol. 2, edited by Giovanni Levi and Jean-Claude Schmitt. Boston: Belknap Press.

Maira, Sunaina, and Elizabeth Soep, eds. 2005. *Youthscapes: The Popular, the National and the Global.* Philadelphia: University of Pennsylvania Press.

Mariátegui, José María. 1988. *Seven Interpretive Essays on Peruvian Reality.* Austin: University of Texas Press.

Martí, José. 1979. *On Education: Articles on Educational Theory and Pedagogy, and Writings for Children from the Age of Gold.* Edited by Philip S. Foner. Translated by Elinor Randall. New York: Monthly Review Press.

Monsiváis Carrillo, Carlos Alejandro. 2004. *Vislumbrar ciudadanía: Jóvenes y cultura política en la frontera noroeste de México.* Tijuana, Mexico: El Colegio de la Frontera Norte.

Munck, Ronaldo. 2000. "Potmodernism, Politics and Paradigms in Latin America." *Latin American Perspectives* 27, no. 4: 11–26.

Nateras Domínguez, José Octavio. 2007. "Información política en estudiantes de primaria y secundaria: Aspectos socioeconómicos y exposición a medios de comunicación:los inicios de la socialización política." *Revista Mexicana de Investigación Educativa* 12, no. 35: 1357–403.

Niemi, Richard G., and Mary A. Hepburn. 1995. "The Rebirth of Political Socialization." *Perspectives in Political Science* 24, no. 1: 7–16.

Nilan, Pam, and Carles Feixa, eds. 2006. *Global Youth? Hybrid Identities, Plural Worlds*. New York: Routledge.

Novaes, Regina, and Christina Vital. 2002. "Today's Youth: Re-inventions in social participation." In *Partnering with Youth to Build a Future*, edited by Andres A. Thompson. Sao Paolo: Editora Peiropolis.

O'Donnell, Guillermo A. 2001. "Democratic Theory and Comparative Politics," *Studies in Comparative International Development* 36, no. 1: 7–36.

Pallares, Amalia, and Nilda Flores-Gonzalez, eds. 2010. *Marcha: Latino Chicago and the Immigrant Rights Movement*. Urbana: University of Illinois Press.

Pateman, Carole. 1976. *Participation and Democratic Theory*. Cambridge: Cambridge University Press.

Piaget, Jean. 1932. *The Moral Judgment of the Child*. New York: Harcourt Brace Jovanovich.

Plato. 1941. *The Republic of Plato*. Translated by Francis MacDonald Cornford. Oxford: Oxford University Press.

Postman, Neil, 1994. *The Disappearance of Childhood*. New York: Vintage Books.

Prilleltensky, Isaac, and Dennis R. Fox. 2007 "Psychopolitical Literacy for Wellness and Justice." *Journal of Community Psychology* 35, no. 6: 1–13.

Prost, Antoine. 1998. "Changer le siècle." *Vingtième Siècle: Revue D'histoire* 60: 14–26.

Putnam, Robert. 2001. *Bowling Alone: The Collapse and Revival of American Community*. New York: Simon and Schuster.

Quijano, Anibal. 1993. "Modernity, Identity and Utopia in Latin America: The Postmodernism Debate in Latin America." *boundary 2* 20, no. 3: 140–55.

Ramos Lara, Eleazar. 2007. "El imaginario político de los jóvenes en México: Notas para su reflexión." In *Política, etnicidad e inclusión digital en los albores del milenio*, edited by Scott Robinson Studebaker, Héctor Tejera Gaona, and Laura Valladares de la Cruz. Mexico: UAM-Iztapalapa-Miguel Ángel Porrúa.

Reguillo Cruz, Rossana. 2004. "Teens at the Border: For a Politics of Representation." In *Teen Life in Latin America and the Caribbean*, edited by Cynthia Margarita Tompkins and Kristen Sternberg. Westport, CT: Greenwood Press.

———. 2005. *Horizontes fragmentados, comunicación, cultura, pospolítica: El (des) orden global y sus figuras*. Tlaquepaque, Jalisco: ITESO.

Reguillo Cruz, Rossana, and Carles Feixa et al., eds. 2004. *Tiempo de híbridos: Entresiglos; Jóvenes México-Cataluña*. Mexico: Instituto Mexicano de la Juventud/ Generalitat de Cataluña/CIIMU.

Reimers, Fernando. 2008. "Assessing Citizenship Skills in Latin America: The Development of a Regional Module as Part of the International Civic and Citizenship Study." Paper presented at the Annual Meeting of the American Educational Research Association, New York, March 24–28.

Rizzini, Irene. 2002. "The Child-Saving Movement in Brazil: Ideology in the Late Nineteenth and Early Twentieth Centuries." In *Minor Omissions: Children in Latin American History and Society*, edited by Tobias Hecht. Madison: University of Wisconsin Press.

———, ed. 2010. *Direitos Humanos de Crianças e Adolescentes: 20 Anos do Estatuto.* Brasília: Secretaria de Direitos Humanos (Federal Secretariat for Human Rights).

Rizzini, Irene, and Gary Barker. 2002. "Promises Kept, Promises Broken: Recent Political and Economic Trends Affecting Children and Youth in Brazil." In *Globalization and Children: Exploring Potentials for Enhancing Opportunities in the Lives of Children and Youth,* edited by Natalie H. Kaufman and Irene Rizzini, 129–50. New York: Kluwer Academic/Plenum.

Rizzini, I., L. Pereira, and N. Thapliyal. 2007. "Percepções e experiências de participação cidadã de crianças e adolescentes no Rio de Janeiro." *Revista Katálysis* 10, no. 2: 164–77.

Rodo, Jose Enriquez. 1961. *Ariel.* Austin: University of Texas Press.

Rousseau, Jean Jacques. 1956. *Emile.* Selections translated and edited by William Boyd. New York: Teachers College Press, Columbia University.

Ruiz Sánchez, Joel. 2008. "El concepto de familia política: Notas para una discusión." *Sociológica* 23, no. 66: 175–86.

Sapiro, Virginia. 2004. "Not Your Parents' Political Socialization: Introduction for a New Generation." *Annual Review of Political Science* 7 (June): 1–23.

Sartre, Jean Paul. 1960. *Questão de método.* Sao Paolo: Coleção Os Pensadores Nova Cultural.

Sassen, Saskia. 1991. *The Global City.* New York: Columbia University Press.

Segovia, Rafael. 1977. *La politización del niño mexicano.* Mexico: El Colegio de México.

Sherrod, Lonnie R., Constance A. Flanagan, Ron Kassimir, and Amy K. Syversten, eds.. 2005. *Youth Activism: An International Encyclopedia.* Westport, CT.: Greenwood Press.

Sigel, Roberta. 1969. *Learning about Politics: A Reader in Political Socialization.* New York: Random House.

———. 1995. "New Directions for Political Socialization Research." *Perspectives in Political Science* 24, no. 1: 17–22.

Silva, I. 2007. "Jovens, estudantes e rebeldes: A construção das memórias estudantis." Paper presented at VII Encontro Regional Sudeste de História Oral—Memória e Política, Nov. 7–9, Rio de Janeiro. ABHO/ Diretoria Regional Sudeste; Casa de Oswaldo Cruz/ FIOCruz (eds.).

Skelton, Tracey. 2010. "Taking Young People as Political Actors Seriously: Opening the Borders of Political Geography." *Area* 42, no. 2: 145–51.

Skelton, Tracey, and Gill Valentine, eds. 1998. *Cool Places: Geographies of Youth Culture.* London: Routledge.

Tienda, Marta, and William Julius Wilson. 2002. *Youth in Cities: A Cross-National Perspective.* New York: Cambridge University Press.

Tirado Segura, Felipe, and Gilberto Guevara Niebla. 2006. "Conocimientos cívicos en México: Un estudio comparativo internacional." *Revista Mexicana de Investigación Educativa* 11, no. 30: 995–1018.

Torres, Maria de los Angeles. 2004. *The Lost Apple: Operation Pedro Pan: Cuban Children in the United States and the Promise of a Better Future.* Boston: Beacon Press.

Tompkins, Cynthia Margarita, and Kristen Sternberg, eds. 2004. *Teen Life in Latin America and the Caribbean.* Westport, CT: Greenwood Press.

Tranberg Hansen, Karen. 2008. *Youth and the City in the Global South*. Blooming-
ton: Indiana University Press.

Tuttle, William M., Jr. 1993. *"Daddy's Gone to War": The Second World War in the
Lives of America's Children*. New York: Oxford University Press.

Tyyska, Vappu. 2005. "Conceptualizing and Theorizing Youth: Global Perspectives." In *Contemporary Youth Research: Local Expressions and Global Connections*,
edited by Helena Helve and Gunilla Holm. Aldershot: Ashgate. 3–14.

UNICEF (United Nations Children's Fund). 2007. *Adolescentes e jovens do Brasil:
Participação social e política*. São Paulo: Fundação Itaú Social–UNICEF–Instituto
Ayrton Senna. Retrieved from http://www.unicef.org/brazil/pt/voz2007.pdf.

United Nations. 2003. *World Youth Report*. Retrieved from http://social.un.org/
index/WorldYouthReport/2003.aspx .

Vinken, Henk. 2005. "Young People's Civic Engagement. The Need for New
Perspectives." In *Contemporary Youth Research: Local Expressions and Global Connections*, edited by Helena Helve and Gunilla Holm, 147–58. Aldershot: Ashgate.

Watts, Roderick, and Constance Flanagan. 2007. "Pushing the Envelope on Youth
Civic Engagement: A Developmental and Liberation Psychology Perspective."
Journal of Community Psychology 35, no. 6: 779–92.

Welton, Neva, and Linda Wolf, eds. 2001. *Global Uprising: Confronting the Tyran-
nies of the 21st Century: Stories from New Generation of Activists*. Gabriola Island,
BC, Canada: New Society.

Youniss, James, and Peter Levine, eds. 2009. "Introduction: Policy for Youth
Engagement." *Engaging Young People in Civic Life*. Nashville, TN: Vanderbilt
University Press.

Zukin, Cliff, Scott Keeter, Molly Andolina, Krista Jenkins, and Michael X. Delli
Carpini. 2006. *A New Engagement? Political Participation, Civic Life, and the
Changing American Citizen*. New York: Oxford University Press.

Two

Chicago Youth Activists

Home Matters in Their Search for Democracy

Maria de los Angeles Torres

Chicago, the third largest metropolis in the United States, prides itself on being a city of immigrants who forged their communities in neighborhoods, workplaces, and churches. The people of Chicago found their political voices through local neighborhood groups, and by organizing to provide for their children's education, safety, and recreation, they became part of the city's civic life. The future of their children was an integral part of their political narratives, so many of their efforts were aimed at youths themselves. Youth organizers and youth-related projects helped form the political and social fabric of neighborhoods.

According to the 2010 census, and the 2005–9 census estimates, respectively, Chicago's population is composed of about 2,695,598 inhabitants, of which 440,214 (or 14.6 percent) are between the ages of fifteen and twenty-four. But young people in Chicago face enormous educational, public safety, and economic challenges. According to the Chicago Public Schools Office of Research, Evaluation and Accountability, 41.6 percent of public school students never graduate from high school. Many young people live in African American and Latino neighborhoods plagued by gang violence and high rates of unemployment.

Chicago is also a city that is deeply divided along racial and class lines, and its communities are clustered around neighborhoods defined by ethnicity and race. Few grassroots organizations have a citywide reach, although there are exceptions. Organizing young people goes on across the city as new immigrants, mainly from Mexico, come to Chicago, and older communities, such as those composed of African Americans, continue to try to make their neighborhoods safer and increase opportunities for their youths. In the past twenty years, organizations have emerged that encourage young people to become active agents of change in their communities and schools.

Who are the young people participating in empowerment projects? How do they engage, and what are their political ideas? This project began by identifying the organizations whose main purpose was to empower youth. The intent was to be broad and inclusive of the many communities throughout the city, as well as of the different forms of civic engagement. The main criterion used to identify the groups was that they be organizations with projects conceived and run by youths themselves (Hart 1992). We began the research by interviewing directors and youth workers in a variety of organizations. They included

- Southwest Youth Collaborative and some of its partnering organizations (Tepochcalli, Interfaith Leadership Project, Multicultural Youth Project, Brighton Park Youth Council)
- Video Machete
- Young Chicago Authors
- Sisters Empowering Sisters (Project of the Girl's Best Friend Foundation)
- Mikva Challenge

The Southwest Youth Collaborative was involved in a citywide school reform project led and designed by students; Video Machete had a group working on a video exploring the impact of the Patriot Act on immigrant communities (the sweeping legislation, enacted after the September 11, 2001, attacks, granted extraordinary powers to the president, gave the government more investigative authority, and severely curtailed civil liberties); Chicago Young Authors was engaged in a program that encouraged the use of the written word to have young people's ideas heard; Sisters Empowering Sisters had a female-run board that gave grants to projects conceived and run by girls; and the Mikva Challenge encouraged youth to work on election campaigns and gave grants to school-based social justice projects conceived and carried out by young people. We asked the organizers, young adults themselves, to help identify other involved youths who were active and interested in participating in this project. The intent was to talk with those who were most active.

Several events that took place before and during the time the interviews were conducted could certainly have influenced an interest in politics (Gimpel, Lay, and Schuknecht 2003). One was the close 2000 U.S. general election, which brought to power a president who had not won the popular vote. This rare political outcome had a profound impact on many young people, who had been taught that the United States is ruled by the voice of the voting majority. There were also widespread concerns about voter disenfranchisement in minority communities. The contested 2000 election was followed by the September 11 attacks and the subsequent invasions of Afghanistan and Iraq. The 2004 presidential election was, again, highly charged, resulting in heightened political interest across the United States and bringing to light the deep political and ideological divides in the American electorate. In Illinois, the 2006 election of Barack Obama to the U.S. Senate (he became the fifth African American senator in U.S. history and the only one in the Senate at the time) provided a unique moment for the state, one that was to have historic implications for the nation (Waldman 2007).

On Becoming Engaged:
Early Influences, Links, and Social Awareness

The Participants

At the time of the interviews, the young people with whom we spoke ranged in age from eleven to nineteen. Of those, seven were males, and eighteen were females. The fact that most were female was not surprising. In many countries, more females than males are involved in these kinds of projects (Flanagan et al. 1998). For the females, gender was an important part of how they defined themselves. Fourteen of the youths we interviewed identified as Latino, Mexican, or Puerto Rican, and about half of those descended from multiple nationalities; eight were African American, although two of those identified themselves as multiracial, in one case African American and Filipina and in the other case African American and Cuban; two were white, and one was Asian American. Youth-related projects tend to be located in less affluent neighborhoods that are seldom majority white. In addition, they advocate for changes that would be more inclusive of marginalized groups and call for a better distribution of goods and services in society. These characteristics are often associated with more progressive politics.

These young activists had a keen sense of self and saw themselves as leaders and agents of change. Carneil (M/16), a member of the Mikva Challenge, said: "I define myself as someone who is open and not afraid to take positions which may not be popular. I feel like I am a born leader, and it is my responsibility to lead, instead of following." Jessica (F/16), also a member of the Mikva Challenge, noted, "You get together and you campaign or you rebel or you do something and things change—you vote—and things change." Noelle (F/16), a member of Chicago Young Authors, also felt that her work mattered: "I can make a difference and I'm cognizant of that, but like I'm just doing it because it makes logical sense to do that—you know, if you don't want this to happen, then go do something about it, you know what I mean?" Samantha (F/15), from Sisters Empowering Sisters, said: "I want to be a light unto this world." Esshan (F/15), from the Southwest Youth Collaborative, also described herself as someone who has hope. Only Jennifer (F/15) had a more altruistic answer, "I got involved because I like helping people."

They also felt that teenagers had strong opinions that should be heard, as Wisdom (F/16) noted, explaining her reasons for joining Sisters Empowering Sisters: "I took the chance because I do have strong views about certain things. I thought it would be an active way to get my ideas heard, and to hear ideas of other girls." The young people also mentioned that most of their peers were not as involved as they were, even though some said that political involvement was becoming a cool thing to do.

A commitment to leadership was accompanied by a sense of responsibility toward themselves and others. Wisdom (F/16) said: "I feel like I have a responsibility to respect myself. I think if more people respected themselves, I don't think a lot of things that are going on would be happening." Some summed up their feelings by saying that they needed to be the best that they could be. Cristina (F/17), a writer with Young Chicago Authors, expressed it this way, "And if I am reckless, not involve others in my recklessness."

Many of the young people we interviewed were children of working-class parents. They had a strong sense of responsibility toward their families. Henry (M/16), a member of Tepochcalli, explained: "My family has gone through some very difficult stages, and it's my responsibility to be there to support them, to try to find solutions, to help my mother out." Esshan (F/15) felt personally responsible for her younger sister.

They also had a sense of social responsibility beyond the home. Noelle (F/17), for example, felt that she had spread her knowledge and interest in art. "I don't think it's promoted enough or not necessarily promoted but encouraged," she explained. "At my school, there's no creative writing program unless you sign up for a creative writing class, and I feel like it's my responsibility to bring things that other people don't have to them."

As much as they saw themselves as leaders, they also admitted that they were inexperienced, and this made them committed to staying informed and to pursuing an education. They watched the news and read newspapers and often discussed politics with friends and family. They were high achievers, many reporting high grades in school, or at least in the classes they liked. And all had plans to go to college. About education, Henry (M/16) said:

I think education is a really big thing; it's a really big responsibility. For me being the first person in my family not going into the military—which I have a lot of cousins that are in the military—having a lot of cousins drop out, and even my younger sister's not looking forward to high school—that's really tough—but I think education is the best way to go, and I'll be the first one to attend college from my first generation here in the United States. So I need to keep up with my education, and hope to be a role model for my family members as well.

Not surprisingly, many of the youths believed that their main responsibilities were related to their political activism. Jo (F/15), a summer intern at the Southwest Youth Collaborative, stated: "I have a responsibility to those who I am organizing with. I signed up to do this; I have to be responsible for what I am doing. Those people are counting on you to be there; just like the people here, they are counting on all of us to work together and get information, get research and try to make a change." Several young people specified that their goal was not just to get involved in politics, but rather to bring about change. Cristina (F/17) felt that she had the "responsibility to share my ideas with others and to promote arts in different places so that others could have the same opportunities I have had in cultural programs to learn how to express themselves."

Political responsibilities included being informed about the world so that they could better act on their beliefs. For instance, Samantha (F/15), from Sisters Empowering Sisters, noted: "I have the responsibility to make sure that I'm not misinformed, because there's such a mass flood of information that the truth gets lost, and you just believe anything and you'll be misinformed and [make] decisions on the wrong thing that can really hurt you." Others felt it was their responsibility to inform others. David (M/16), of Young Chicago Authors, said, "I think that my responsibility as a youth who knows about so many inequalities and so many injustices is to educate others, and to build the movement, because I think that is the most worthwhile thing I can do with my time." Daisy (F/19), of the Brighton Park Youth Council, added that voting was important: "Really, it is a right, not a responsibility, but you should do it." Jesse (M/17) saw that it was his responsibility to keep elected officials accountable, "especially if we helped elect them."

Family

Earlier approaches to socialization sought to find ties between childhood development and political attitudes and ideas (Flanagan and Sherrod 1998; Easton and Dennis 1970; Greenstein 1965; Hess and Torney 1968; Connell

1971). For adolescents, socializing institutions included the family, schools, and peers (Jennings and Niemi 1974). For urban youth, these institutions, as well as experiences of violence and injustice, can contribute to their desire to get involved (Ardizzone 2007). The young people were asked about early influences, how they got involved, and what motivated them to stay engaged. Of the twenty-five young people interviewed, only two had parents actively involved in political activities. Maceo (M/13), a member of Video Machete, thought that his parents' involvement was a gift, and he felt blessed. Cristina (F/17) and Noelle (F/16) recalled being taken to political events by their parents, although they were not necessarily activists. Many non-immigrant parents voted and made it a point to instill in their children a sense of duty in casting a vote. This was especially true for the African Americans, whose parents taught them that the vote had long been denied to their community, and so there was a historic responsibility to vote. In most families, politics was a common topic of conversation, even if the parents themselves were not activists (Jennings and Niemi 1981). Maceo (M/14) recalled: "We talked politics at dinner all the time. My parents would give me a book to read, and we would discuss it, and then they would give me another one."

But while activist parents were the exception, one experience the participants all seemed to share was that they had a parent at home who respected them and their ideas, listened to them, and let them speak up and express their points of views. It was not so much that politics and political activism were encouraged, but rather that they were respected as individuals. Jessica (F/17), one of the youths from the Mikva Challenge, explained: "I was the first kid and grandkid in my family, and because of that I was never treated like a kid. I was never told, don't do that; rather, go ahead, do it." Noelle (F/17) recalled, "My parents have strong political opinions, but I always felt that, even if we disagreed, they still took my opinions into consideration. I was allowed to express mine."

Not all parents wanted their children involved in politics. Indeed, in some cases, parents counseled against it for a variety of reasons, including the feeling that political activities would take them away from their studies. Immigrant parents worried that their children's political activism would draw the attention of the government to the members of their family who were undocumented. The parents of Vianny (F/16), of the Interfaith Leadership Project in Cicero, were fearful that if she became involved, something could happen to them. But as far as she was concerned, they encouraged her, since they figured she knew more about U. S. society than they did and knew what she was doing. In those situations, youths reported that they felt respected by their families. After all, said Terri (F/17), a young Cambodian

5. Undocumented and unafraid. Photo by Amalia Pallares.

refugee, "We know the language more, and we were brought up here." The fact that they spoke English and had more knowledge of U.S. society made them brokers between their private familial context and the public sphere. In effect, that gave them a special status within the family. And in some cases, immigrant parents *were* very supportive. Mayra (F/18), of Tepochcalli, thought that perhaps because her parents could not vote, they encouraged her to do it, "so their voices will be heard, too."

Other youths attributed to their families the values and traits that led them to activism (Flanagan et al. 1998). Jennifer (F/15), from the Southwest Youth Collaborative, said: "I pretty much follow the beliefs that I was taught when I was little." Samantha (F/17) gave her mother credit for teaching her: "My mother gave me all the tools I needed. She was very open with me. I'm an only child, so she's very open with me about everything . . . there was nothing that I couldn't do, nothing that I couldn't accomplish if I put my mind to it." Jessica (F/17) said that her parents gave her a strong will. Gisela (F/15), a member of the Interfaith Leadership Project in Cicero, remembered that when she was little, her grandfather taught her the importance of giving back to people by reading her stories of good Samaritans.

Those who did have politically involved relatives said these relatives had encouraged them to follow in their footsteps. Lindsey (F/16), a member of the Chicago Coalition against the War, explained, "I think, for me, the trigger was the declaration of war on Iraq. I knew in my mind that this was not a good way to do it, that this wasn't the right thing, that Iraq wasn't really a threat to the United States, and that we were just creating more violence when we didn't have to. I have a lot of political history in my family. My aunt and uncle were both in Students for a Democratic Society [an activist student group of the 1960s], so I sort of got a little inspiration from them."

Institutions outside the Family

While self-esteem and values were formed in the family, most on the young people in our project became involved as adolescents, and schools and peers played a critical role in their engagement (Jennings and Niemi 1974). In addition, given the great disparities in social capital across communities, institutions outside the family were important influences in their political involvement. Some mentioned teachers who had introduced them to civics issues. For instance, Henry (M/16) and Omar (M/17), from Tepochcalli, talked about one teacher at Farragut High School in Chicago's Little Village neighborhood who had taught a special class on law and politics and had spent a lot of time with students after school. "He taught us about laws, and what our rights are." Mayra (F/18) said she learned about Tepochcalli in her law class, adding: "that's where I started getting involved with politics." Civics teachers in some Chicago public schools worked closely with the Mikva Challenge to get students to identify issues facing them and set up programs to address these issues.

Many of the young people had held leadership positions in school organizations such as student councils, math and science clubs, and black student unions. In particular, debate clubs, where students learned to articulate and research positions, were training grounds for political activism. Carneil (M/16), from the Mikva Challenge, said: "Debate teams taught me how to think politically and order my thoughts, and allowed me to meet people from all over the state, from rich suburbs and poorer school districts."

Schools also engaged students intellectually and provided knowledge that developed critical thinking that could lead to social action. Jennifer (F/15) noted: "I started to read the book *Hiroshima*. That got me more into politics and the way things work, and when Bush won, and Gore didn't, and Gore got more votes and everything, I was like, now, wait a minute, how could he have gotten more votes and he lost? And when 9/11 happened, even before that, I got up and started to look at my surroundings, and think about what I could do to try to change some of the things that I didn't agree with."

Outside the schools, community-based youth organizations provided a place for activism and a site for students to develop skills, allowing young people to feel empowered and respected. As Jessica (F/17) explained:

Mikva, it's an organization that doesn't tell you what to do. They have a certain plan that they want you to follow, but everything is up to you. They don't treat you like children. Their belief is that "if you kids are serious enough to do this and to give all your time to this, then we're going to trust you." So they really have a lot of faith in the youth, and that's what I really loved about them, and then I stood with them and I kept doing similar things.

Agreeing with that idea of support, Maceo (M/13) said: "I think Video Machete gives a venue for me to say exactly what I want to say, uncensored." Terri (F/17) also felt that, in her community organization, she could finally speak her mind:

Youth, especially in the Cambodian community, don't get a lot of voice. They say, "I'm your elders, shut up, listen to me, obey me." It's really cool that I found this program, cause I would've been into the whole,

"Yes mother and yes uncle, I agree with everything you say." But being heard, being outspoken, has taught me that I have a right to be heard and people will hear me whether they like it or not, and you will respect me as much as I respect you.

In their projects, the youths found they had enthusiastic and supportive community organizers who taught them important political skills, including surveying, lobbying, and writing press releases (Ginwright, Noguera, and Cammarota 2005). Most important for many of the participants, the organizations introduced them to other young people from across the city and taught them how to listen to them.

Few youths expressed that they were influenced by role models, and for those who did, almost none of these models were politicians. The only exception was Barack Obama, then-aspiring U.S. senator from Illinois, whom some defined as a person they could believe in. Carneil (M/16), who worked on Obama's Senate campaign, recalled: "I found a great inspiration and role model in Barack Obama. I think that he stands for a lot of the issues, and he can communicate them and give practical solutions."

Early political victories also encouraged optimism about social activism. All three young people from Cicero's Interfaith Leadership Project were excited about all the programming they would be able to provide after persuading a local businessman to donate a building to their organization. Those involved in Obama's campaign for the Senate were ecstatic about his victory. "This showed me that someday I can be a senator too," said Carneil (M/16). A group from a community in Chicago's Brighton Park had been involved in a campaign that resulted in the election of an alderman who was not later responsive to their needs. This only seemed to make them want to work harder. "We helped get him elected, and he turned his back on us," recalled Jesse (M/17) a member of the group. "Now we have to find a better person."

Religion, although identified by most as a family practice, did not seem to play a significant role for the youths we interviewed. The exceptions included two Muslims, Esshan (F/17) and Jo (F/15), from the Southwest Youth Collaborative, who felt that their value system was encoded in religious text, and Cristina (F/17), who had gone through the initiation rites of Santeria. For her, religion was a centering experience that allowed her to reach out to others.

Schools and community organizations seemed to play similar roles to those noted by other scholars (Andolina et al. 2001). As noted earlier, the young people we interviewed learned useful skills, particularly on debate teams and in classes, although most of them were also involved in other school organizations that allowed them to develop leadership and organi-

6. Mikva students and Barack Obama. Photo by Mikva Challenge.

zational skills. But schools were also contested zones. Youths often referred to them as the place where they lost their voice or the place that did not prepare them for the future. Mayra (F/18), for instance, said she had rights as long as she was not on school property. This may stem from the fact that many Chicago schools have responded to gang violence with extraordinary vigilance that includes metal detectors, locker searches, and even body searches. In contrast, community organizations were the places where young people met other committed youths and where they learned political skills. These organizations provided stimulating political environments in which budding activism could find a more collective expression. Through community-based activities, young people began to feel empowered as youth and as informed citizens. Meeting young people from other communities encouraged them to be more open and forthcoming in accepting others who were different from them. Other researchers have also found that these organizations become safe zones in which young people feel that they can be themselves (Halpern, Barker, and Mollard 2000).

Social Awareness

Politics is often played out as a group process. Social identities frequently demarcate political groups, and ethnicity and race have also been used to keep groups from having a political voice (Tienda and Wilson 2002). In the

United States, only white male property owners of a certain age were considered part of the political community when the Constitution was written in 1787. In the past two hundred years, struggles to expand the polity have succeeded in bringing in African Americans and women, and they have also resulted in lowering the voting age to eighteen. Many of those movements were organized along the same social categories that had been used to exclude groups from the political process, giving rise to "identity politics." Identity politics has been part of the modernist politics in the United States as groups have sought to broaden notions and practices of citizenship (Young 2002).

For many of the young people interviewed, awareness of shared characteristics was an important first step in becoming part of a social group. The prevalent social categories identified as important by the youths included age, race, ethnicity, and gender.

All of the young people interviewed had a special awareness of their status as *youth*, and some thought that because of this, they brought special sensibilities to the political process because of their age. They felt they had power when they were working with a youth organization and with other youths. Terri (F/17), who was born in Cambodia, felt that as a Cambodian she was expected to play certain roles she found demeaning to women. For that reason, she said, "I don't see myself as part of the Cambodian community, but I do think [of] myself as part of a youth community, really a member of the activist youth community." Carneil (M/16), a young African American, summed up what he had learned at the Mikva Challenge: "Youth have a voice and the power to effect change. Youth make up a constituent, when we shop, buy clothes, or go to the corner store, we pay taxes and some have jobs. When youths come together and have a vision, a good leader, they can definitely change a lot of things." The young people felt a sense of community and belonging in their organizations. David (M/16), from Young Chicago Authors, explained: "Organizing youth is worthwhile because youth have opinions, and just because you are in high school doesn't mean you can't think." The young people felt that they could make a difference when they acted together. As Jo (F/15) said, "I don't think they would listen to me, but if I had like a more powerful group behind me, or something, maybe they'd be more responsive."

In addition to age awareness, race and ethnicity also demarcated a sense of group and self (Sanchez-Jankowski 2002).This awareness was especially true of African American and Latino youths. Carneil (M/16) felt that it was a privilege to be an African American male: "I feel that the rights that I have to affect things right now are going to be great, because I feel as long as I stay on this track, I can go directly to the top. I believe that mindset can lead me to understand and not forget."

For Latinos, the issue of ethnic identity becomes more complex because they can choose among multiple categories (Padilla 1985; Montero-Sieburth and Villarruel 2000). The Latinos interviewed usually defined themselves first by their national origin and second as Latinos. Jessica (F/17), from the Mikva Challenge, defined herself as Mexican even though she was born in the United States: "It is a way of carrying on my parents' and grandparents' heritage. I want to keep it going." Jennifer (F/15), from the Southwest Youth Collaborative, said, "I am Puerto Rican, I don't deny it, but I don't rub it in people's faces. We are all humans, and we all have needs."

However, *Latino* was the primary identifier for Luis (M/16), from the Southwest Youth Collaborative, because for him, "Mexican did not sound right. I grew up over here, and I am totally different than they are. I would call myself Latino." For others, the term *Latino* was used strategically as a way of uniting and not offending others. An example of this was expressed by Gisela (F/15), from the Interfaith Leadership Project in Cicero, who used the term as a conscious choice to avoid excluding anyone: "I'm Latina and really proud to be Latina, and I don't like saying I'm Mexican. I mean, I'm completely proud of being Mexican, but it's kind of like I don't want to say you're Mexican and cut all others." Daisy (F/19), from the Brighton Park Youth Council, defined herself as "a minority youth." adding: "Now, from there, I'd describe myself as someone with a goal." Choosing *minority* implies that she sees herself as part of a larger community of Latinos, Asian Americans, and African Americans.

For whites, an affinity for black culture helped them understand privilege and inequalities and the deep divides in their own world. David (M/16) remembered when he started listening to hip-hop. "A lot of hip-hop is involved with the African American community," he explained. "All my friends were white; I started thinking, well, it shouldn't just be like that."

Gender is also a powerful social category, an important component of the young people's identities and one particularly tied to age. The girls from Sisters Empowering Sisters had an interesting take on their identities: "We are girls, not little women."

The identity references for women of color were multiple. Wisdom (F/19) described herself as follows: "Afrocentric. And I use woman too. I think being a woman is beautiful. And minorities. Being a minority is even more beautiful. White women are beautiful, too, but I just take pride in who I am. That's what you have to do without being influenced by others. Whether you're a man or a woman, white or not." Noelle (F/17) defined herself as "a multiracial girl who's gone to private school her whole life. I define myself as a writer, as a student. I'm one of those intellectual types, but I also like to sit in front of the mirror for hours—I'm a teenage girl."

Discrimination and Activism

As empowering as group membership may be, many of the young people were also aware that they faced discrimination precisely because of their age, race, and gender. However, instead of creating obstacles to their activism (Ginwright 2006), those aspects of their identity became a reason for their involvement, because they saw a connection between the way they were portrayed and their lack of voice. They also sensed that these images affected the ways that they are spoken to and treated.

Gisela (F/15) described her experience in Cicero, a working-class suburb west of Chicago: "Our reputation of youth is not very good. If you're over five feet tall, you cannot be in a park. If three young people are walking together at a corner, they can technically be arrested because it's three of them, and it's a gang and all this stuff."

Race awareness also includes becoming cognizant of discrimination. Maceo (M/13), from Video Machete, explained: "When I was younger, race was not relevant. I did not know what color I was. I knew we ate different foods at home, that you rolled the r's in our last name. Until I started hearing words, racial slurs, and started to understand what they were, why some people got to do something and others not. And why some people in class got yelled at more than others."

Maceo defined himself as Afro-Cuban-American. But he was frustrated because people tried to pigeonhole him into one or the other of his identities:

> These people have ideas of what I'm supposed to be, and I'm not fulfilling those ideas of what I'm supposed to be like. And it's strange, and I'll argue with them about the ideas they're talking about. And now, I'm seen as being an aggressor; I'm seen as being angry, or that I hold a grudge against white people.
>
> You can't be in the middle. I've dealt with this also because I'm Cuban and I'm black. And they have problems with that, because I'm light-skinned, but I'm black. And they can't deal with that because I don't fit their little perception of what a black kid looks like. And they have a problem with me being Afro-Cuban, for that matter, because I don't look like I'm from the barrio.

The "American" identity was missing from their self-descriptions, especially for Latinos who rejected it even if they were born in the United States or were naturalized citizens. Luis (M/16) said he never referred to himself as American: "I'm not. I don't have a big pride for Mexico, but I'm Mexican and not ashamed of it." Mayra (F/18), from Tepochcalli in Little Village, said, "I came to the United States at three. I don't want to be American, because when I think of American. I think of the American dream, and this is unattainable. It's just a dream. America has failed minorities." Daisy (F/19) expressed similar feelings: "The American dream—it's not that much glory. When I think of American, I think of the American dream. And you know what, to me, it's there, it's attainable if you don't die trying, but they don't make it accessible to you."

Young women confronted special stereotypes. For them, gender inequities within their religion and society were barriers to becoming a full member of society. Esshan (F/17), who is a Muslim, explained: "In my religion, they separate girls from boys. The older I get, the more this becomes an issue. This is not preparing us for real life." Others were bothered by the effects that stereotypes have on the ability of girls and women to get ahead. Samantha (F/17) said:

> I feel strongly about women and how we can do so many things and how sometimes, especially teenage girls, we allow stereotypes to put us in little itty-bitty boxes as to what we can do or what we should do. You shouldn't be loud, you shouldn't be sexual, you shouldn't be outspoken a lot of time, you shouldn't push the envelope, you shouldn't question things, and I just feel that's not how you learn. You have to push the envelope to learn about the world and about yourself.

Racial profiling and targeted repression by the police tend to affect young people disproportionately, especially in immigrant and African American communities. Some of our participants had personal experience with this. As Gisela (F/15) noted, Cicero has ordinances that prohibit more than three young people from gathering in public spaces. More than 90 percent of youths in Cicero are Latino. She added, "It is a law that targets us."

Several of the young people, though, were aware that while they might be specific targets because of their age and background, their entire community was also repressed. Henry (M/16), from Little Village, said, "The cops in my community have power over certain people because they are not citizens, and many do not know their rights." Jennifer (F/15) acknowledged "that it was not just young men or young women, or kids, who have no say, 'cause most of the people in this community are undocumented or have migrated, so they're barely trying to work up the ladder. But it's not that easy, so they might be in the same place for a while, and a lot of people, they stereotype. Oh, those damn Mexicans, they're lazy, good for nothing, and stuff like that." Luis (M/16), from the Southwest Youth Collaborative, said: "I hate to go back to the Latino thing, but it exists. There are a lot of people who have more power than Latinos, and they ignore them. They don't know we exist, historically or otherwise. This leads to the abandonment of the community and its needs, and as such it becomes a rallying point." This sentiment was also expressed in terms of equal opportunities and rights for neglected communities, including African Americans, gays, and lesbians. They shared a strong feeling that they were not treated equally.

This realization reflects a sense of responsibility to their families and communities and is tied to a desire to change unfair situations. Henry (M/16), from Little Village, said, "What really motivates me to get involved is my family, the problems that my family has, deep down inside the family, the financial problems, other things. I don't want them to continue facing hardships, and I want to help and change the things that affect them, and not just for my family, but [for] other families in the communities who have similar problems."

Social awareness of discrimination does not only come from a sense that the youths and their communities are treated differently because of their age, race, ethnicity, and gender. The young people also see negative stereotypes about themselves in the media (Grossberg 2001), where they are often portrayed as uncaring and apolitical and, if they are African American or Latino, violent as well. Omar (M/17) said, "Youth of color are portrayed as gangbangers . . . stereotypes make it very hard to work yourself up the ladder."

The effects of these stereotypes were clearly perceived as obstacles to being considered full and intelligent members of a civic community. Noelle (F/17) said, "They dumb down the news for us because they think that youth are uncaring and not interested."

The awareness of a need to change cultural representation was also accompanied by an understanding that youth were part of a larger community and needed to represent a constituency. For some, it was the youth community for which they felt responsible. Cristina (F/17) explained: "I'm responsible for myself, but I have to take into account my actions and how they will be perceived by others, because it will affect how all youths are perceived." She also believed that she had "the responsibility to the people I represent, other young people and Latinos, to other women, and people who practice my religion, other writers. In other words, I need to be a role model." She added, "I feel strongly that my responsibility is to change the image that others have of young people."

Others were influenced by their gender and racial and ethnic backgrounds. Noelle (F/17) explained, "I feel like I have the responsibility to change the image people have of teenagers in society and in the media. I feel like I have the responsibility to represent black people. I feel like I have the responsibility to represent my parents. I have the responsibility to represent myself. You know, I think my responsibility basically is to maintain my image and make it seem really good." Samantha (F/17) said, "I have responsibility to represent women, represent black women, intelligent black women, strong black women. I feel I have the responsibility to represent black people, to represent my parents and myself." Lilian (F/13): "I don't want to be pitied as [a] little Mexican girl. I want to show them I can be just as smart."

Jennifer (F/15) believed that stereotypes can be broken down through action:

> The fact that we have an organization where youths want to try to change our schools, instead of adults trying to do it for us, that makes us seem like we're more responsible and we actually care, instead of like the whole stereotypical thing where kids nowadays don't care, all they do is sit in front of the TV. When we go against the assumption, and it gives us a voice, I think that's power right there. The power of breaking down perceptions.

We found a link between awareness of discrimination and activism. There were references to cultural and gender-based identities, and cultural representation was integral to the politics of these young people. Social identities were not necessarily the defining dimension for the organizations in which these young people chose to participate, as was the case for many activists of the 1960s (Muñoz 1989). Concerns about racism and discrimination were central to their engagement, even as they defined their youth groups by age and activity.

Engaging: Issues, Practices, and Place

In this section, I describe the issues important to the young people interviewed as well as the ways in which they engaged (C. Cohen 2005). Their issues can be described as "sites" of activism, since it is through them that they engage and locate their advocacy.

Education

Even though those interviewed came from different parts of the city and from a variety of organizations, the issue that most engaged them was education. Their concerns included curriculum, lack of resources, not having a voice in school affairs, and the unequal distribution of educational resources in the state of Illinois.

Some of the youths said that educational services and resources were the most critical problems affecting them. Some mentioned funding. One mentioned how overpopulated schools were and how little teachers could get done since there were so many students. The students from Southwest Youth Collaborative were working on a summer-long project to try to get more resources, particularly college counselors, for their high schools; without more counselors, they felt their access to universities was limited. Dante (M/11), from Video Machete, said that he felt sorry for his teacher, who used her own money to buy supplies for her students. He felt that she should get a higher salary.

Others pointed to the lack of equitable distribution as the culprit for unequal education. Carneil (M/16) was especially keen on this issue: "For

7. Mikva students and Chicago Public Schools superintendent Jean-Claude Brizardt. Photo by Mikva Challenge.

young people right now, a major battle is the inequitable distribution of funding for Illinois. Some suburbs receive more funding per pupil versus inner-city urban schools because of the property taxes, which is mainly where the revenue comes in." He felt this was inherently unfair and undemocratic. Mayra (F/18), from Little Village, summed up her feelings: "I don't think we really have democracy. We don't get equal rights. Our public schools are not funded as well as suburban schools; we are not seen as equals." Within the city, there are great disparities between magnet schools and other schools. Terri (F/17), of the Multicultural Youth Project, commented on this: "We have a two-tiered system of education; one in the magnets, and another for regular schools. And only a few can get into the magnets." Her group had met with Chicago School Board officials and was in the process of producing a video to depict these disparities.

Even in schools with special programs, which were set up to offer better educational opportunities than regular schools, there are issues of inequality. Sabura (F/14), a Lincoln Park High School student and a member of Girl's Best Friend, talked about how the International Baccalaureate (IB) and honors students were treated in contrast with student in the regular program: "I asked a teacher to let us read a book that was being taught to the IB students, and she said that we could not read that book, only the IB students could read it. It is so unfair."

For many of the students, not having a voice in the decisions that affect them was the most serious problem in their education. Jennifer (F/15), who lives on the southwest side of the city, put it this way: "Everyone talks about educational changes, but they are adults. We are the ones who are in school, and we are the ones affected by decisions, so they should count on us. It would make us more responsible for what is going on in our schools."

Others felt that school policies were too restrictive. For instance, Luis (M/16), of Southwest Youth Collaborative, was working on a campaign to gather support for students to change a rule called Zero Tolerance, which mandated that students be automatically suspended after their first infraction. Students from Farragut High School in Little Village had been involved in a walkout to protest school conditions. Mayra (F/18) felt that when she was in school, she lost rights. "We have rights outside of school because we are citizens, but once we get inside the school, they take half our rights away. Our privacy is gone and so is our right to protest." To a large extent, the concerns voiced by these young Chicagoans are present in other cities as well (Pizarro 2005), as is the sentiment that fighting for equal education is a way for students to organize in order to better their communities (Bhimji 2005).

Another important set of issues had to do with the ways young people are misrepresented in popular culture. Noelle (F/17), from Young Chicago Authors, thought that cultural representation was one of the most significant parts of politics. She was involved in a project to create alternative images by encouraging young people to write and perform poetry that addressed class and race discrimination. Mayra (F/18), from Tepochcalli, helped organize events to invite parents and community members to hear what teenagers were doing in their communities. Of these activities, Henry (M/16) reported: "One particularly rewarding experience was bringing together the parents of the youth in our organization and having them involved, and at the same time having them recognize the importance of the work their children were doing." These activities eventually led to forming a group, and Omar (M/17) explained that the first three letters in the acronym SIYOLEAN, which they used to name the group, stood for Stop Ignoring the Youth and that Olean "was Nahuatl for 'movement.'"

Sister Empowering Sisters had a program to teach girls about philanthropy and fundraising. A board of girls aged fourteen to eighteen was given money for organizations that had programs for girls and run by girls. The girls on the board were working a video to show how the media's portrayal of girls was taking away their voices. Video Machete participants were being trained in filmmaking and were working on films portraying their immigrant communities. These projects gave young people a chance to have their voices heard.

Electoral Arena

As is the case with young people in other parts of the country, only a few of the young people we interviewed had, as their primary commitment, the electoral process (Strama 1998). That group was involved with the Mikva Challenge and the Brighton Park Council. For Jessica (F/17), working on elections was a way of changing things:

> I never had the view, "Oh, politics is bad. They never listen to the people," or anything like that. My family always voted. I basically felt, "Well, there's good guys, and there's not so good guys, and you just gotta pick which one you wanna work for."

The young people of Brighton Park had been very involved in local electoral campaigns, which they saw that as a way to make changes in the community. They supported one candidate who promised to help open a

8. Mikva students working on electoral campaigns. Photo by Mikva Challenge.

recreation center. After he was elected, he ignored the youth group. Daisy's (F/19) response was, "Well, we will have to find another candidate to run against him in the next election."

While many were not directly involved in elections, they understood the importance of voting, and those who were old enough to vote, did. For instance Wisdom (F/19) shared the following:

> When I turned eighteen, it wasn't the big election for president. It was the primaries. It was kind of cool because everybody was like "Vote!" So I feel you should vote. As opposed to, you shouldn't vote. Because people have done a lot for you—women, and African American, and Latinos—to vote. You should vote. I just think there should be better people running for office."

Of particular importance to many were meetings with public officials during which they could present their cases and argue for changes in policies. These encounters left the lasting impression that through hard work and informed politics, they could make changes in the political system. At the least, they could stand up and be heard.

Immigration

In recent years, the United States has been embroiled in a national debate about immigration reform. In 2006, pro-immigrant advocates organized the largest-ever marches in the United States. The first one was in Chicago, and young people were an integral part of that movement (Flores-Gonzalez and Pallares 2010). Immigration issues directly touch the lives of Latino youths. Their advocacy for more humane immigration policies and for equality for immigrants comes from experiences they and their families have had. Lilian (F/13), from Video Machete, who was working on a film about the impact that the 9/11 attacks had on immigrant communities, recalled her family's stories: "I interviewed my father. He was telling me how difficult it was. He immigrated with eleven brothers and sisters. They didn't have beds to sleep in. And they didn't have dinners to eat every night. They ate like scraps and slept [on] the ground on *colchones* (mattresses), and it was horrible. And how they got caught once and got sent back." Maceo (M/13) was also working on that project: "The focus of that workshop was to look at immigrants or first generation [Americans] and have them find where they belong and their identity and understand who they are."

The young people also believed that immigration was an important part of the history of the United States. Omar (M/17), of Tepochcalli, said: "Some of the people in the government forgot that the United States was built on immigration. America is built on many cultures colliding into one." Mayra (F/18) echoed those feelings: "The white people are immigrants, too. They think that this is their country, when this doesn't belong to nobody but the Indians, the Americans, the natives."

In particular, many of these young people mentioned the Dream Act, the proposal that has many versions including a state one that would guarantee access to higher education to any student who graduates from a U.S. high school, regardless of immigration status. Many of the youths had lobbied their representatives to pass this bill in the state legislature.

Concerns about immigration policy extended beyond its direct impact on those youths. Many felt that Muslim Americans were being unfairly targeted, especially after 9/11, by federal immigration officials. The group working with Video Machete spent the summer of 2003 on a project looking at the impact of the Patriot Act. Others felt there had been a spillover effect into their own communities, as they believed 9/11 had become an excuse for the federal government to target all immigrant communities. These actions heightened existing racism against immigrant communities. For Luis (M/16), from the Southwest Youth Collaborative, "it is racism to deny someone a job because he is Mexican and has no papers. But this has been happening more and more." Terri (F/17), who had become a refugee at the age of five and had spent several years at a camp before coming to the United States, said, "I don't understand the concept that one person can tell another that they are illegal." There was consensus among the young people that immigrants should be granted citizenship. Carneil (M/16) said: "I don't know a lot about immigration itself, and letting people come over the border or anything like that, but I do feel that anybody who lives here, or most people who live here, should have rights to go ahead and vote, because they're affected by it."

The War

The 2001 invasion of Afghanistan and the Iraq War were playing a prominent domestic role during the time of the interviews. While only one of the young people interviewed defined herself as principally an antiwar activist and was a member of an antiwar organization, many were critical of the wars and questioned their logic. Others were concerned about their impact on young people. And still others felt that the United States was imposing its will on others.

Lindsay (F/16), who was a member of Chicago Coalition against the War, explained her position: "Some wars are inevitable. World War II was one. But this war was unnecessary. I supported going into Afghanistan because I believed that they were helping Osama bin Laden, but what does Hussein have to do with 9/11? Nothing." She had helped organize speakers at her school and had joined with a broader citywide coalition to organize protest marches and voter registration drives of people who would oppose the war.

Dante (M/11), who was part of Video Machete, helped organize a protest against the war at his school. For him there was something inherently illogical about the war: "The president sent out tanks that used up a lot of oil for gasoline, just to get more. This wastes a lot. I don't think it is right to sacrifice a lot of lives just to get a substance to save the country. You know, we could get solar-powered cars." Lilian (F/13), from Video Machete, had helped organize a walkout in her school. She said, "This whole war is a grudge. Instead of killing people, Bush should have sat down with Hussein and worked things out. He needs to listen to the U.N. that said not to go to war. Now there is a war, death, and the economy is failing." Lindsay (F/17) aid, "The war has brought military recruitment down, and the Defense Department is pressuring recruiters. They go out into poor communities with promises of education and training. Instead of helping them get into a university, they are telling them to go to the military."

Luis (M/16), whose two closest friends were in Iraq, was ambivalent about the war, but felt that the troops needed to be supported. But Samantha (F/17), from Sisters Empowering Sisters, who had two brothers in the army, said: "I'm one of those people who do not believe in this war. I don't think lives should be sacrificed. The world can work with not everybody being like America. Who are we to say what is freedom to them? I do understand that Saddam Hussein did inflict pain and suffering, but I am saying so many lives don't have to be sacrificed. Maybe there were other ways to bring about changes."

Envisioning: Their Political Ideas

For young people, political activism means confronting an unfolding set of beliefs and ideas about their place in society, their rights, and their notions of citizenship. Yet they also have clear ideas about what kind of government they would like to have. Even as their politics are locally grounded, they have a sense of themselves in relationship to the rest of the world.

Rights

The young people in our study were asked what rights they felt they had. Their answers unveiled notions of rights overwhelmingly embedded in law and in the Constitution. All felt strongly that they had the right to express themselves. "I have the right to be heard and respected," Cristina (F/17) said. Lilian (F/13) believed that she had a right to say what was on her mind: "I have a right to use my voice. I have the right to the First Amendment, the freedom of speech, and the freedom to practice religion." Carneil (M/16) added an element of political responsibility to his right of speech. "I am gifted with a voice. And the reason I have a voice is to use it. And I am not limited to where I can use it. However, I have to figure out when to use it most effectively." Gisela (F/15) added that her rights were "basically get involved and know everything that's going on and try to make the changes that need to be changed."

The young people also felt that they had the right to participate in governmental decisions and to contest and protest in order to hold politicians accountable. Noelle (F/17) explained: "I know that I can protest; I can rally; I can, more than anything, I can always ask questions and challenge authority. That doesn't mean beating on people, but I know that I can always have a dissenting opinion that is mine."

Maceo (M/13), in particular, felt that dissent was part of being a good patriot:

9. Mikva students at the Illinois State Capitol in Springfield. Photo by Mikva Challenge.

Especially after September 11th there was a push toward patriotism. And patriotism is getting changed—I think that's the problem as I see it. On a large scale, patriotism is being turned into something which is more connected to the military, and fighting. And not toward community and caring, I guess, more about people. Also, people who don't completely go along with everything the government does become unpatriotic, and in my opinion, they're the deepest patriots.

Activism has made these young people aware of the ways in which they can exercise their rights. For example, when Carneil (M/16) traveled to Springfield, the capital of Illinois, he met Rep. Michael Madigan, the speaker of the Illinois State Assembly. The experience made him understand that, if armed with data and oratory skills, he could stand up and present his case.

As strongly as these young people believed in their right to free speech, they also extended this to others, even those with positions they did not condone. With regard to racist speech, Maceo (M/13) said: "I think it's sad that people believe in those things, but again, it's not my place to tell them, 'This is what you have to believe.' It's not my place to tell them how to run their lives. And if they want to go through life believing that they are the supreme race or that other people are under them, it's none of my business, as long as they don't come after me."

The only social right mentioned by some of the young people was the right to what one called "a fine education." Maceo (M/13) also thought that everyone should be entitled to medical care.

Many of the students, however, acknowledged that their rights were limited, and that they were not entitled to hurt others. They also believed that they had the right to protest, but they needed to be respectful. Mayra (F/18) added: "Rights are abstract. When it comes to organizing in schools, for instance, I can't do that without risking getting kicked out." They also felt that many of their rights were limited because of their age, especially the right to vote.

Some felt that although they might have rights in the public sphere, as long as they were living at home, their rights were circumscribed by their parents. Dante (M/11), who helped organize a school walkout to protest the war, was warned by his mother not to walk out himself because it would be disrespectful to his teachers. "I have the right to organize a protest, but then I have to listen to my mother," he said. While understanding certain limitations, clearly they felt that there were a series of personal rights to which they were entitled. These included how they could dress and talk, the right to introduce themselves to others without masking who they were, and the right to choose their friends. In addition, many had deep feelings about their personal liberties. Young women, in particular, felt strongly about their rights over their bodies. Noelle (F/17) said: "I feel like I'm entitled to all the rights in the Constitution, but I also feel like I'm entitled to the right to dress however I want." Wisdom (F/19) added, "I have a right over my body, of course, which I think every woman does."

More Democratic and Socially Responsible Government

A few saw politics as something outside their reach and felt government and politicians had the power to control their lives or at least have an impact on them. Some felt that government only represented the rich. While some of the youths did not see themselves as part of government, they liked to think they could influence governmental decisions. In discussing formal politics, Dante (M/11), the youngest person interviewed, believed that elections could hold politicians accountable: "Just government would be one in which politicians are held accountable to their voters, not the president. And a higher level of consciousness and morality would help."

Governments were not seen as entities unto themselves, but rather as political processes that were defined in different ways. Maceo (M/13) believed that the "ideal politics would probably mean looking at, and critically analyzing and deconstructing, the world, and being conscious of what's going on. And making sure what you feel is heard, and that other people's feelings are heard. And I think politics should be going toward making life for people, everywhere, a better place."

For Lindsey (F/16), a good government is one that respects the rights of the people, gets the people involved, and makes sure they have a say in what goes on. A good government protects the rights and liberties of the people, but also makes sure that they carry out their responsibilities. Generally, good governments were described as responsive, transparent, and honest.

About inclusion in formal political communities, they were divided. Some viewed their fellow classmates as uninformed and not caring. Since being informed was such an important aspect of their political culture, they thought that those who were uninformed should not be allowed to participate. But for some, the question of age was not critical. They felt that by age sixteen, most youths could make informed decisions. If you are able to drive, why not vote? For Jessica (F/17), the issue was straightforward: "Since governmental decisions affect everyone, then everyone should be involved somehow, including children."

Latino youth, in particular, thought a good government would be more inclusive of immigrants. Mayra (F/18) noted: "You know, the United States has forgotten that it was immigrants and slaves that built its greatness. Immigrants need to be included; after all, they are the ones who work the hardest." Omar (M/17) thought that "ideally we would put a lot more faith in working-class people, not just rich ones; it should be about people." Wisdom (F/19) echoed this sentiment. Government, she said, "should be more diverse. In sum, a democratic government would include everyone. Not just old men. Put in some women, black women, some Latinos. Young people as well."

These youth activists believed that government had a role to play in providing services, particularly to needy communities. Maceo (M/13) explained, "I would like to see health care for everybody and a good education. In my ideal world, I would like a society built on principles in which people had the ability to live with dignity, to have certain control over their lives, not to be powerless. Where there was a better distribution of wealth, and government was there to make sure that some people are not falling under, like medical insurance of some kind." Daisy (F/19) said: "I don't think we should have a

10. Chicago youth jobs rally. Photo by Mikva Challenge.

different form of government. I don't want communism, I don't want, you know, a dictatorship. But our democracy, it just doesn't seem to be equal, and it doesn't seem to include everyone."

Place of the United States in the World

Our participants had global points of references in that they were aware of the plight of young people in other countries. Those who had traveled abroad also understood that there were marked differences (Helve and Holm 2005; Nilan and Feixa 2006). There was an awareness that they lived in the most powerful country in the world, and because of it, they felt a sense of responsibility to make sure that the United States did not abuse its power or ruin the environment. There was also a sense that a powerful country had responsibilities to weaker ones. For instance, Omar (M/17), from Little Village, said: "I would like to see the United States help other countries, not go to war with them. To help them build up their economies. So they would not be poor."

The young people also felt that human connections should be taken into account when making policy. Some, like Jennifer (F/15), believed that the war was wrong because it overlooked human ties. "The people in Iraq or Afghanistan, they are human beings; they've got feelings; they've got families, just as we do, and it seems like they don't take that into consideration."

Their empathy is conditioned by an understanding that there are differences. Luis (M/16), from the Southwest Youth Collaborative, said: "I think we don't understand poverty as it is experienced in other parts of the world." Samantha (F/17) noted: "I think I'm different from other youth in other countries in that I was raised here in America, where it seems that we were taught to be a superior country." Another difference mentioned between their political culture and that of many other countries was that they did live in a society that permitted dissent, even if it was often muted.

Jo (F/15), from the Southwest Youth Collaborative, saw similarities between U.S. youths and those in other countries: "Youth from all around the world have one commonality: wanting to love and be loved—even when there are other differences." "In an ideal world," Jennifer (F/15) said, "I would try to get all these different types of people to come together and realize that we are the same; we are linked in this world."

The young people also wanted a world in which they were taken into account in the present. Jessica (F/17) explained: "I want a world in which people had faith in students, because we are the ones getting education." Cristina (F/17), the young poet, said: "In my ideal world, my stories would affect people, because people will listen more to people who look like me. In an ideal society, I would be heard." And Daisy (F/19) added: "We're working for a better tomorrow, but why not have it today?"

Note

This project was partially funded by the W. K. Kellogg Foundation and through a fellowship at Chapin Hall. I would like to thank Dolores Muñoz, Phoebe Connely, and Nawojka Lesinski for their research assistance. Special thanks also to Roger Hart and Caitlin Cahill for their thoughtful comments on field notes from this research project, published in *Children, Youth, and Environments* 17, no. 2 (2007).

References

Andolina, Molly W., Krista Jenkins, Cliff Zukin, and Scott Keeter. 2003. "Habits from the Home, Lessons from School: Influences of Youth Civic Engagement." *PS: Political Science and Politics* 36, no. 2: 275–80.

Ardizzone, Leonisa. 2007. *Gettin' My Word Out: Voices of Urban Youth Activists.* Albany: SUNY Press.

Bhimji, Fazila, 2005. "Latino/a Youth Contest for Equity in the Public School System in Boyle Heights, Los Angeles: A Political and Theoretical Perspective." In *Contemporary Youth Research: Local Expressions and Global Connections,* edited by Helena Helve and Gunilla Holm. Hants, UK: Ashgate.

Cohen, Cathy. 2006. "African American Youth: Broadening Our Understanding of Politics, Civic Engagement and Activism." In *Youth Activism: A Web Forum*

Organized by the Social Science Research Council. Retrieved from http://ya.ssrc.org/
african/Cohen/.

Connell, R. W. 1971. *The Child's Construction of Politics.* Carlton, Victoria: Melbourne University Press.

Easton, David, and Jack Dennis. 1970. *Children in the Political System.* New York:
McGraw Hill.

Flanagan, Constance, Jennifer Bowes, Brita Jonnson, Beno Csapo, and Elena
Sheblanova. 1998. "The Ties That Bind. Correlates of Adolescent Civic Commitment in Seven Countries." *Journal of Social Issues* 54, no. 3: 457–75.

Flanagan, Constance, and Lonnie Sherrod. 1998. "Youth Political Development:
An Introduction." *Journal of Social Issues* 54, no. 3 (Fall): 447–56.

Flores Gonzalez, Nilda, and Amalia Pallares. 2010. *¡Marcha! Latino Chicago and
the Immigrant Rights Movement.* Urbana: University of Illinois Press.

Gimpel, James G., J. Celeste Lay, and Jason E. Schuknecht. 2003. *Cultivating Democracy: Civic Environments and Political Socialization in America.* Washington,
DC: Brookings Institute Press.

Ginwright, Shawn, 2006. "Toward a Politics of Relevance: Race, Resistance and
African American Youth Activism." In *Youth Activism: A Web Forum Organized
by the Social Science Research Council.* Retrieved from http://ya.ssrc.org/african/
Ginwright/.

Ginwright, Shawn, Pedro Noguera, and Julio Cammarota, eds. 2006. *Beyond
Resistance: Youth Activism and Community Change: New Democratic Possibilities
for Practice and Policy for America's Youth.* New York: Routledge.

Greenstein, Fred. 1965. *Children and Politics.* New Haven, CT: Yale University Press,

Grossberg, Lawrence. 2001. "Why Does Neoliberlalism Hate Kids? The War on
Youth and the Culture of Politics." *Review of Education, Pedagogy, and Cultural
Studies* 23, no. 2: 111–36.

Halpern, Robert, Gary Barker, and William Mollard. 2000. "Youth Programs as
Alternative Spaces to Be: A Study of Neighborhood Youth Programs in Chicago's
West Town." *Youth and Society* 31, no. 4: 469–506.

Hart, Roger A. 1992. "Children's Participation: From Tokenism to Citizenship."
Innoncenti Essays no. 4. Florence, Italy: UNICEF.

Helve, Helena, and Gunilla Holm, eds. 2005. *Contemporary Youth Research: Local
Expressions and Global Connections.* Aldershot, Hants, UK: Ashgate.

Hess, Robert, and Judith V. Torney. 1968. *The Development of Political Attitudes in
Children.* New York: Transaction Press.

Jennings, Kent, and Richard Niemi. 1974. *The Political Character of Adolescents.*
Princeton, NJ: Princeton University Press,

———. 1981. *Generations and Politics: A Panel Study of Young Adults and Their
Parents.* Princeton, NJ: Princeton University Press.

Montero-Sieburth, Martha, and Francisco A. Villarruel, eds. 2000. *Making Invis-
ible Latino Adolescents Visible: A Critical Approach to Latino Diversity.* New York:
Falmer Press.

Muñoz, Carlos. 1989. *Youth, Identity, Power: The Chicano Movement.* New York:
Verso.

Nilan, Pam, and Carles Feixa, eds. 2006. *Global Youth? Hybrid Identities, Plural Worlds*. New York: Routledge.

Padilla, Felix. 1985. *Latino Ethnic Consciousness: The Case of Mexican Americans and Puerto Ricans in Chicago*. Notre Dame, IN: University of Notre Dame Press.

Pizarro, Marcos. 2005. *Chicanas and Chicanos in School: Racial Profiling, Identity Battles, and Empowerment*. Austin: University of Texas Press.

Sanchez-Jankowski, M. 2002. "Minority Youth and Civic Engagement: The Impact of Group Relations." *Applied Developmental Science* 6, no. 4: 237–45.

Strama, Mark. 1998. "Overcoming Cynicism: Youth Participation and Electoral Politics." *National Civic Review* 87, no. 1: 71–77.

Tienda, Marta, and William Julius Wilson. 2002. *Youth in Cities: A Cross-National Perspective*. New York: Cambridge University Press.

Waldman, Paul. 2007. "The Youth Vote, the Culture Wars, and Barack Obama." *American Prospect*. Retrieved from http://prospect.org/article/youth-vote-culture-wars-and-barack-obama.

Young, Iris Marion. 2002. *Inclusion and Democracy*. New York: Oxford University Press.

Three

Affirming the Young Democracy
Youth Engagement in Rio de Janeiro

Irene Rizzini and Malcolm Bush

The Context of Youth Civic Engagement in Brazil

The backdrop for contemporary youth's civic engagement in Brazil was a series of events in the country's recent history that aroused unheard of levels of political participation (Rizzini and Barker 2002). In 1989, the first direct election for the presidency of the republic was held after twenty-one years of military dictatorship. In 1993, the nation's political passions were aroused again by the financial corruption of the democratically elected president, Fernando Collor de Mello, who was impeached and removed from office. His removal followed massive street demonstrations against him by, among others, student activists. In 2002, Luis Ignacio "Lula" da Silva—the head of the Workers Party (PT), the most significant progressive party in Brazil–was elected president after three unsuccessful attempts at running for that office. These events were the result of—and themselves permitted—a new type of political and civic engagement in the country.

In Brazil, to be engaged in the critical decades of the 1960s and the 1970s, according to the Brazilian anthropologist Alzira de Abreu (2000), meant participation in the struggle for a more just society. Early in that struggle, the search for a more just society depended on overthrowing the military dictatorship and installing a democratic regime. The members of the so-called leftist movements—among whom were the Brazilian Communist Party (PCB) and the Communist Party of Brazil (PC do B)—and the revolutionary guerrilla movements came together for this purpose at the end of the 1960s.

In the past several years, young people have received special attention in the Brazilian political agenda. Several sectors of society—including young social movements, organizations of civil society, and the federal government—have engaged to improve daily conditions and opportunities for youth. Their most notable achievements were the passage of a National Policy for Youth and the creation of the National Secretariat for Youth (SNJ), the National Council of Youth (CONJUVE), and the National Program for the Inclusion of Youth: Education, Training, and Community Action (ProJovem).

The National Secretariat for Youth is part of the Brazilian president's General Secretariat and is responsible for integrating all the federal government's programs for young people, paying special attention to the characteristics and diversity of youth. The Secretariat is also the reference point for federal youth policy at the state and municipal levels.

The National Council for Youth includes government officials engaged in youth issues, as well as organizations and experts concerned with young people and with public policies involving them. It has sixty members, forty of whom are from civil society and twenty from the federal government. Its purpose is to propose policies for young people and to promote studies about the socioeconomic realities that confront them.

The situation of young people in Brazil is of great concern partly because of their large numbers. The 2003 United Nations Report on the World Population lists Brazil as the country with the fifth greatest percentage of young people (ONU 2003). According to data in the Report on Youth Development, in 2007 there were 35 million young people in Brazil between the ages of fifteen and twenty-four. Data from the Brazilian Household Survey 2006 (PNAD) listed 2.5 million of those young people living in the Rio de Janeiro metropolitan region.[1] Moreover, 29 percent of the fifteen- to seventeen-year-olds in Rio, and 21 percent of the eighteen- to twenty-four-year-olds lived in households with incomes below the poverty line.

One troublesome statistic about Rio's younger population is the reduction in the number of black and brown youths (*pretos* and *pardos,* respectively, in Portuguese—the Brazilian census requires respondents to identify themselves by color) in the city between 1993 and 2003.That fact is most likely related to the high levels of violence and homicide that are most pronounced among nonwhite youths. A report sponsored by the Brazilian government to mark the twentieth anniversary of the passage of the pathbreaking Statute on the Child and the Adolescent notes an increase in the murder rate of young people twelve to eighteen years of age in Brazil, from 18.7 per 100,000 in 1997 to 24.1 per 100,000 in 2007; the majority of the victims were black and brown (Rizzini 2010). International comparisons in youth homicides show a vast difference between Northern and Southern Hemisphere countries. The publication *Mapa da Violencia: Os Jovens da América Latina* (Map of Violence: The Young People of Latin America) (RITLA 2008) shows homicide rates for youth (young people aged ten to twenty-nine) of 51.6 per 100,000 in Brazil, 73.4 in Columbia, 1.7 in Portugal, 12.9 in the United States, and 10.4 in Mexico. As with figures on poverty, youth homicide rates vary enormously by race, region, and city. The rates of homicide for black males in the city of Rio de Janeiro reach the horrifying rates of 300 per 100,000. *The Twenty Years of the Statute* reports rates twelve times higher for males than for females and twice as high for blacks and browns as for whites (Rizzini 2010).

Brazil has now achieved an elementary school registration of about 95 percent, a huge improvement over figures at the end of the dictatorship. School attendance, however, still fluctuates considerably. There has been some improvement in Rio in high school attendance, although the quality of the public schools is still a cause for great concern. In Rio de Janeiro in 1993, about 13 percent of young people had attended or completed high school. In 2003, that figure exceeded 20 percent. Partly as a result of this increase in students pursuing secondary education, there was a reduction in the number of young people in the workforce. In the Rio de Janeiro metro area, black youths, however, were more active in the labor force than their white counterparts because of economic pressure to contribute to the incomes of their families.

The unequal distribution of educational and occupational opportunities among blacks and whites is high throughout Brazil, but it is higher in Rio than in the country as a whole. That fact is reflected in the patterns among the young people who study and who do or do not work while they are attending school. The number of black youth who only study is much smaller than that of the white group, and a much greater percentage of black youth only work. One factor that has a direct impact on the percent of young people who only study is income. The greater the family income, the greater the number of young people who only study (Bush 2008). Family background also has an impact on school achievement. Among the youths who do attend school, lower-income children, males, and young people whose parents cannot read or did not complete elementary school are much more likely to be two or more years behind grade level than others; those characteristics are also associated with skin color. Brazil's high level of income inequality (one of the highest in the world) and the concentration of low-income urban families in slums or *favelas* create a huge divide in the living situations and life chances of Brazilian youth.

Engaged Youth in Rio de Janeiro

Our study examines in detail the engaged youth in the Rio de Janeiro metropolitan region. Such a sample raises the question of the general levels of involvement of young people in Rio and in Brazil as a whole. According to the Brazilian social scientist Paulo J. Krischke (2004), current studies of Brazilian youth indicate a strong interest in conventional politics and engagement in unconventional political activity.

A random sample survey conducted by the Institute for Religious Studies (ISER 2002) in the Rio de Janeiro metropolitan region concentrated on the social, civic, and political participation of youth. This survey, which included eight hundred young people between the ages of fifteen and twenty-four, discovered some interesting facts about how they participated in the city. Most of the youth in this study (70 percent) were participating or had participated at some point in their lives in groups associated with churches. Forty-two percent of the young people attended church at least weekly, and 62 percent at least monthly. However, young women participated more than men in church groups, while young men participated more in student groups (48 percent of the sample participated in student-organized activities). Ecological and community organizations also attracted young people (20 percent); traditional political organizations, such as trade unions, interested them less (10 percent). About 8 percent participated in nonprofit organizations. The survey also investigated questions about young people's political activity, ascertaining that most of the young people (56 percent) would vote even if the vote were not mandatory. The degree of determination to vote was directly related to educational levels: the higher the educational level, the greater the wish to vote.

Another relevant study, but with a national scope, is entitled *Brazilian Youth and Democracy: Participation, Spheres and Public Policy* (IBASE and Instituto Pólis 2005). This random sample of eight thousand young people (nine hundred of whom also participated in group interviews) covered the seven metropolitan regions in Brazil and the federal district of Brasilia and included young males and females between the ages of fifteen and twenty-four. The researchers interviewed the young people about participation in political, social, and community activities because of the importance of those activities for strengthening Brazilian democracy.

The study showed that about one-third of the young people were engaged in groups, organizations, or movements. The study further discovered that it was the youth with more years of schooling who participated the most. The main activities in which they were engaged were those related to religion (42 percent of the young people who said they participated in any group), sports (32 percent), and cultural activities such as music, dance, and theater (27 percent). And although only 8 percent considered themselves to be politically active, most of those interviewed showed an interest in political issues. Eighteen percent of the young people said they participated in activities or movements for improving conditions in their neighborhoods or cities, a finding that is useful for putting the sample in our own Rio study in perspective.

Another study that examined political participation by Brazilian youth, released by UNESCO in 2006, was *Youth and Young People: What Unites Them and What Separates Them?*[2] The objective of this study was "to contribute to the consolidation of an agenda that treated in the most careful way the question of youth in Brazil." Among other things, the study focused on the political participation of young people; their perceptions, values, and ideas; sexuality; sports, leisure, and culture, and their opinions about using legal drugs as well as the consumption and legalization of illegal drugs.

The youth in the UNESCO sample reinforced the conclusions of the other studies we have described in that the groups or movements to which

11. Staging a play in Rio de Janeiro. Photo by Manuelle Rosa.

the young people were most connected were the church (69 percent), followed by the student movement (48 percent), the ecology movement (20 percent), community work (17 percent), political parties (10 percent), and volunteering in nonprofits (8 percent). In 41 percent of the cases, the direction or administration of the organizations in which the youth participated was in the hands of adults, while 34 percent of the time it was in the hands of young people. In 24 percent of the organizations, the responsibility was shared. This means that in more than half of the organizations the young people had at least some responsibility for the decisions of the organizations.

These surveys show a variety of activities in which Brazilian young people engage. While each study sampled different groups, there were some striking similarities in the responses. Church activities, for example, are a common form of participation. Particularly in low-income communities, where violence is common, the church is seen as a safe place to meet and also a place where people find some support and a sense of belonging. Moreover, church-related groups traditionally carry out charitable or social projects aiming at helping those most in need and often specifically targeting young people. In addition, some religious groups in Brazil have been engaged in political action, such as the struggle for agrarian reform. Churches were very active in the struggle against the dictatorship.

The Rio de Janeiro Participants

The sample construction for this study took place in three stages. In the first phase, our team worked with another project called Cultures of Participation, which had been initiated a few months earlier at our research center. In this phase, the researchers identified eleven organizations that worked with youth and had as part of their mission the promotion of participation and a sense of citizenship. The groups supported a variety of cultural and community activities (Butler, Princeswal, and Silva 2007). Semistructured interviews were conducted with the coordinators and several professionals from those organizations to identify especially active young people.

In the second phase, twelve young people from these organizations (ages sixteen to twenty-seven) volunteered to participate in the study. They were interviewed individually from May to July 2006. From this group, eight also agreed to work on personal narratives about their participation. From July to December 2006, this smaller group held monthly meetings with members of both research teams to share their narratives and to work together on writing a book.[3]

In the third phase, we interviewed another fifteen young people from September 2006 to June 2007. Because we had made the decision with the Chicago and Mexico City partners to have a top age limit of twenty-four, the three older youths were excluded from the final sample, completing a group of twenty-four youths from the city of Rio de Janeiro. Since the Rio researchers had decided to find some young people engaged in political and religious activities to broaden the scope of the analysis, we picked this second group mostly from such organizations. We constructed the group by asking colleagues and the young people already in the sample to introduce us to others. From this second group, another eight young people wrote their own narratives. The sample is, therefore, constructed to include those known by NGO leaders and their peers to be civically engaged and to have participated in a variety of civic activities.

The sample then comprised twenty-four young people between the ages of fifteen and twenty-four, of whom fourteen were female and ten male. Eighteen of the young people were nonwhite, and six were white. Fifteen were low-income, and nine were middle-income. In addition to interviewing young people who lived in *favelas* and in middle-income neighborhoods, we interviewed young people who belonged to the Movimento dos Trabalhadores Rurais Sem Terra (Landless Workers Movement, or MST).[4] One young person in the group had completed only elementary school, sixteen young people had attended or completed high school, and seven had attended college.

The kinds of organizations in which the young people were engaged can be briefly described as follows. Ten were involved with political parties and social movements (the regular parties, student movements, and the MST). Eleven young people took part in social and cultural projects. These projects included community radio, youth and human rights, gay rights, rap (*consciência negra*, or black consciousness), hip-hop, and dance or theater, and a group involved in a program that trains low-income youth for the nationwide Brazilian university entrance exam, the *vestibular*. Three others were connected with church groups including Catholic and evangelical organizations.

In the next three sections, we discuss the stories of engagement. We first focus on their narratives of how they got engaged, their motivations, and who influenced them. In section two, we discuss what forms their engagement took. In section three, we focus on their ideas about youth in general and their participation in society, as well as in their related beliefs and views of the world. But before we discuss the patterns in their responses, we should echo one young person's warning that the collective term *youth* hides many legitimate differences in behavior and views of the world:

We shouldn't forget to talk about the differences between different groups of young people. So to talk about youth without thinking about these differences, which are not social in the general sense but are still differences among youth. . . . You can't generalize when talking about youth, the particular characteristics of each young person, the diversity of youth. (Leo, M/17)

On Becoming Engaged:
Early Influences, Links, and Social Awareness

When we asked young people to describe what they remembered about how they started to engage in civic activity, most were articulate about their initial involvement. One group of respondents could be said to have a natural inclination to be active, to mobilize others, and to lead others. Some of them began their involvement in school and church when they were still children, as in the following examples:

> I have always been very engaged, always enjoyed participating, in school activities and also in the church. I was only 9 when I started engaging, and now I teach in this church. (Joana, F/17)

> When I was 13 years old, I started taking the responsibility as coordinator of "Mãe Rainha" for the church.[5] It involved thirty families. It is a group of people, and everyone was over 40 years old. I took the responsibility for over a year, and now I am one of the youth leaders. (Alexandra, F/17)

Others began their participation as student leaders, as elected members of committees or councils whose purpose was to represent the students' interests. It became clear through the interviews that young people took these roles seriously. Pedro (M/20) said:

> I was active in my school since eighth grade. This was because I saw there were so many problems: lack of funds from the government, lots of strikes. It was a conscious participation.

Jessica (F/18), who was active as the president of the student association on the state level, declared:

> I always wanted to organize myself to participate, to be part of the struggle, mobilizing students, until I had a chance. I got elected, and since then, I go to sleep late, wake up early, and spend all day out.

Another group exhibited an internal restlessness that led them to action. Some of the young people referred to the fact that, as children, they were rebellious and competitive. Jonas (M/20) said:

> I have always been like this. My mother used to say:"You are a very rebellious boy." I have always been a fighter [someone who does not accept things as they are] looking at things in a critical way.

This spirit was exhibited in children from all socioeconomic backgrounds. Fernando (M/24), who used to be a street child and is now the leader of a community radio station, said: "I always had this desire for change inside me."

This desire for change seems to be a fairly common characteristic of young activists. Krischke, a social scientist, observed, "There is enormous optimism on the part of young Brazilians in believing that they can change the world, attributing to their personal efforts and capacity to innovate the achievement of a better future for their own lives, their neighborhoods and the country they live in"(2004, 22, 23).

Several young people expressed a sense of unease that seemed to come from the fact that they felt different from the people around them. They felt the need to look for different ways of expressing themselves and to search for groups of people like themselves. Miriam (F/20) noted: "I am very different from my parents. I used to feel like a fish out of water, because they are very different from me; we have different views about life." Mateus (M/24), member of the Landless Workers Movement, said: "I am very far from my childhood friends. We belong to very different realities."

A last group found people and spaces that facilitated and encouraged their participation and activism. Several of the young people began in settings that supported them in the exercise of leadership, in expressing their ideas, and in becoming actively involved. Often the stimulus came from the example of their parents and from of friends who were already engaged.

Jonas (M/20) and Luciano (M/20), two activists who were interviewed together, noted:

> We started participating together when we enrolled in the same school. It looks like we've known each other for a long time, but it is not true, we started engaging together. We had met these other guys from school student council who had good ideas. They were organizing a demonstration to press the local City Hall to get free bus fare for all students from public schools. They pressed us to participate to help many others, they said, and that is how it all started.

Motivations for Engaging

The young people we interviewed had different reasons for becoming engaged. They mentioned religious, political, familial, personal, ideological, and practical motivations. Different motivations could inspire the same young person at different times. Most of the young people in the sample became engaged out of the urgent wish to participate in society, to do something concrete, to be useful, or to help others. These responses seem to come out of a sense of restlessness and indignation motivated by a deep social awareness:

> This is what I think: Society is the most important thing one has. So to participate in society is to work so that this society becomes a bit more just, less unequal. (Leo, M/17)

> All our advances [e.g., all the progress achieved by humankind], if we don't do it in favor of the communal, if we don't have the perspective of the community, of the demands of solidarity, will continue in individualism; in a little while, we won't have a planet left, you understand? This is the issue. (Miriam, F/20)

Fatima (F/20) said:

> When you do something good to others, you feel good yourself. It is not just a favor you are doing, but I think, well, I don't know, I think we human beings look for a meaning in life.

The word *help* was used quite often in the interviews. For some, helping had a political meaning. Mateus (M/24) remarked:

> To participate is to build. It is to insert oneself in the social environment and help the process of constructing society. This is what it is to participate.

Fernando (M/24) saw participation in an altruistic light: "To work, man! We must always be working, helping the person next to us, doing good."

For a few young people, participation was linked to altruism; helping was an altruistic gesture associated with a religious motivation. The young woman who told us about her participation as the coordinator of the novena when she was only thirteen also shared with us that she had feared she would not be able to accomplish her mission, but that she knew she was right in helping others and that she trusted "the saint was guiding her."

For several of the youths, the act of participating gave them a meaning in life and a place in the world. This was particularly true for those who felt discriminated against. Patricia (F/22) said: "The hip-hop movement gave me a direction in my life regarding the racial issue, an understanding of what I want from now on."

Many of the young people affirmed a dream to contribute to changing those things in the world that offended them. A good example was given by Jonas (M/21), who said:

> When you participate, you are helping in some way; you are helping to change something tomorrow, for example. When I took part in the political campaign, I think I made a difference, I added something.

Mateus (M/24) echoed that sentiment:

> To participate is a form of transforming society. I think that the students' movement is fair and crucial. But it does not solve the problem. What we need is the transformation of society. With a movement with this conception, one can transform the world.

Several showed a passion for what they did, speaking about a personal commitment and participation. Marcia (F/16) affirmed that to participate

> is to give of your best so that what you are engaged in works out well; to do all that you can and beyond that. If you can jump, you jump. If you fall, that act of falling shows people that this experience, too, is part of life. So I think it is about giving totally of yourself.

Finally, some talked about that moment when they made themselves heard and realized they had participated in something important. Two young people had very moving stories about that feeling. The first, Leonardo (M/24), who had taken part in a gay rights demonstration, said:

> And so, when I looked in front of me and saw that crowd, I had not seen all those people. I had been engaged in the task, I had seen nobody around me. And then when I breathed and saw a million people, I thought, My God! I am part of this, I have succeeded and I wept. I had helped make this happen. And it worked.

Gabriel (M/23) was equally emphatic:

I guess what most moved me was when I realized that I was really participating in the history of Brazil. It was when I got my voting card and when
I voted for the first time in 2002, for the presidency. I was so emotional
and I felt that I was truly taking part in society.

This young man came from an extremely poor family, on the margins of Brazilian society, who took great pride in participating in the civic act of voting.

The testimony of this group of young people demonstrated a strong desire
to work in some way for the common good. Both the young people from
middle-class families and those from poor families showed that they were
connected, that they were present, that they cared about the state of society,
and that they struggled to make their dreams and aspirations for society
come true. They made it clear that they benefited from this participation.
They became better able to express themselves in public, better prepared
to act, and their voices were heard and respected. Finally, there is no doubt
that they developed a strong sense that change involved a struggle, and that
they were no longer passive but active participants in their society.

Who Influenced Them?

We also wanted to learn who influenced the young people in their activist
careers. We found that for most of the participants the influence came from
a person close to them or from people they admired. Most said that they
were influenced by their own family, particularly their parents.

In writing his personal narrative, Felipe (M/19) said:

I go back, however, to my childhood and to the decisive influence my
parents had in this process. It was impossible for me not to remember
my father's constant struggle as a public servant to improve conditions
at the Hospital for State Public Employees, of his work with the doctors'
union, and his defense of political democracy as a way of improving social
conditions. My mother, although in a different way, had showed me early
on that we were a privileged minority in an unjust and unequal society.

Alexandra (F/17) remarked: "My family, too, was always very Catholic, and
so the encouragement of my mother was crucial."

Peers were also important. Our respondents often mentioned friends or
colleagues who were already engaged in an activity and ended up introducing
them to a specific group. Some referred to events or a specific phenomenon
that attracted them—for example, a course, a book, or an activity related to

a political party. But even in these cases, there was someone who served as a reference. There was, for example, the story of Leo (M/17), who was inspired when he heard a judge talking about the Brazilian Children's Rights Act (the Statute on the Child and the Adolescent). He mentioned the event to his father, and then his family encouraged him to learn more about it. As a result, he got engaged with a group of activists who worked for a nonprofit organization dedicated to the human rights of young people.

Raquel (F/15), who volunteered with the Youth of the Brazilian Democratic Party, reported:

> I could say that it was Father [who influenced me] because he introduced me. Like it or not, it is an influence. Basically, he introduced me to the topic and I liked it. If I had wanted to leave, he would not have put any pressure on me to get engaged. The fact is that I liked it, and I grew. And today, he can hardly believe that I am so engaged.

The influence from friends was present in many stories. Some mentioned longtime friends, among them Denise (F/16) and Fatima (F/20), below:

> It was a childhood friend of mine, T, who was already in the group (a theater and dance group) for some time. Her mother knew that I liked to dance because I had danced in my grandmother's backyard in the mirror. I was not able to see a mirror without dancing. So she said that one day she would take me there, and she took me and I watched a performance, a group of young girls, and I went another day and I kept on going until one day when I had my first performance. I was not able to leave. I couldn't leave there again.

> I had a friend from church, A, who herself is a very determined person. She helped me so much, and always believed in me. She always told me, "You have potential, you must discover this," and it was she who suggested my name to the coordinator, and she always gave me good advice.

These two statements tell us something else that is important in the development of youthful activism: engaging in activities at the community level. According to Juan E. D. Bordenave, "Participation in the community level is the best preparation one can have to participate as a citizen at the level of a global society" (2002, 58). It was also, for many young people, the natural point of contact with civil society.

Some respondents had been influenced by people who did not belong to their family or community circles:

What influenced me was the struggle of [the Brazilian politician] Leonel Brizola.[6] He was always so slandered, but for me he was a figure who deserved admiration. (Leo, M/17)

My main reference was the camp [of the Landless Workers Movement] because, after all, I was in the camp for five years, and it was really that experience that helped me a great deal. The camp taught me a lot. The courses, the study that I did were just a complement. What really taught me was being at the camp for five years. Whatever book that I read today, whatever course of study I have done, whatever program I have graduated from was a supplement to what I lived in the camp. All this within this new social structure, which is being organized by the workers. It was fundamental. I am speaking about the camp, the whole situation, the families, the leaders. (Mateus, M/24)

The school setting was also a significant source of influence for young people, and in addition to their peers, teachers and professors were also important mentors.

A few young people in our sample said that no one had influenced them. Fatima (F/20) was emphatic in saying that the idea to become engaged was her own:

Mine, totally mine. Besides, there is no one in my family involved in politics, nor a professor . . . no one. I am a surprise!

Brazilians scholars have pointed to certain factors that promote and inhibit participation. The presence of an authoritarian father or a submissive mother, for example, could contribute to the raising of children accustomed to obeying out of fear or respect, as they avoided opposing the rules laid down by their parents. On the other hand, participation could be facilitated through the actions of a leader who believed in listening to everyone's opinion as an instrument for constructing solutions to the problems in the community.

In our study, we came across accounts of barriers or limitations to youthful participation created by adults. Sometimes, parental influence was ambiguous. Jonas (M/20) described how his parents, though supporting the development of his social conscience, sometimes discouraged him from participating in student movement activities. Both had been activists, and because of their actions they had been forced to move from one city to another so that they would not suffer reprisals. Luciano (M/20) reported that although young people encountered daily financial difficulties in participating in the student movement (for example, to buy meals and to pay for travel from one school to another), some middle-class parents would not assist their children's activism. But many parents were supportive. We finish this section with the story of Pedro (M/20), who thought himself unjustly treated. He had been suspended by the director of his high school for going from classroom to classroom to summon students to a meeting of the student council. In this account, the young man's parents came to his defense:

> I was already an adult and was 19 years old when the director called my parents. This was already a mistake, but we went to see him and talked. And he began to say that I was a bad student and such things. And then they agreed. But when he talked about my moving from one classroom to another, my parents defended me. They said, "You can always visit a room as a student whenever you like; in that, we will support you." And that this director, they said, he is indeed a fascist.

Engaging: Issues, Practices, and Place

In this section we describe the activities and organizations in which youth in Rio were involved, and we discuss what they told us about their participation. Since some of the young people were involved in a number of groups, we categorized them according to what they said was their most important current activity. Raquel (F/15), for example, was an active member of an important political party in Brazil; she participated in the student movement in her school and was also very active in her church, where she was responsible for teaching and organizing activities such as plays, training courses, workshops, and job opportunities for other young people. Fatima (F/20) had leadership positions both in a political party and in the student movement, where he held the position of treasurer of the Brazilian Union of High School Students.

What links most of these youths is their sense of responsibility toward others in society and their engagement in activities that allow them to feel they are "doing something," or as several told us, that they are not passive. The different forms of participation they report can be understood, according to several authors, as including traditional and more contemporary forms of civic engagement.

The political scientist Lucio Rennó, in a 2003 study focusing on political opportunities and engagement in civil society in Latin America, mentions two kinds of traditional engagement: participation in associations on a national level, such as political parties and trade unions, and participation in

12. Protesting urban removal in Rio de Janeiro. Photo by Manuelle Rosa.

"local social groups" (Rennó 2003). The form of participation that involves advocacy on a national level requires clear and specific objectives and the mediation of collective interests. This definition can be applied to the first group of our youthful respondents—those engaged in political parties, student movements, and the Landless Workers Movement. The second form of participation defined by Rennó refers to collective action at a more local level. Forms of local participation can be traditional, such as in church groups with a religious, social, or cultural focus; or they can focus on more contemporary issues, such as gender or racial and ethnic rights.

Whatever the form of civic activity, young people's participation depends on the existence of local groups or networks, which are often the first to arouse the interest of young people in the broader civic society.

Types of Civic Activity

The activities in which the young people were engaged were, of course, shaped by the organizations and their purposes. Those engaged in political parties were in most cases responsible for organizing a number of activities

related to young people. Their activities as leaders of the youths in their parties (*juventude do partido*) ranged from canvassing to engaging other youth
locally or nationally to organizing events such as meetings, assemblies, con-
ferences, and training courses.

Those involved with student movements describe their organizations'
mission as improving public education and fighting for equal educational
opportunities both locally and nationally. The activities they mentioned
included visiting schools to strengthen the local student committees (*grêmio
estudantil*), or to create such a committee in schools that did not have one,
and organizing meetings and events to demand better education.

Those connected with social and cultural projects reported a variety of
activities, including dancing, singing, and playing musical instruments in
cultural groups. Those characterized as social projects also displayed a diversity of forms of activism, such as running educational and mutual support
workshops, marching in parades, and distributing condoms in the port district of Rio with a gay rights group. These groups aimed to raise awareness,
particularly among young people, of human rights' violations. The young
people expected that these activities would lead to social change.

13. Performing a protest play. Photo by Manuelle Rosa.

Those who were active in church groups reported clear responsibilities for other young people, particularly children. They worked hard to engage children in after-school activities in church settings, teaching them such skills as acting and dancing and often teaching catechism. Some had leadership roles working with other youths or with poor people, or caring for the saint to whom the church was dedicated and organizing novenas for devotional groups.

Many of the youth had executive responsibilities. For example, Miriam (F/20), who ran the program to prepare low-income students for the college entrance exam, planned the program, delegated the tasks, and monitored the staff. She also ran the local community newspaper, where she made assignments, conducted interviews, took photographs, and edited and rewrote the articles. Both the treasurer and the secretary of the Brazilian Union of High School Students visited schools to start student committees and to strengthen existing groups.

Degrees of Involvement

The extracurricular activities reported by the youths require different degrees of initiative and involvement. For example, joining a youth group is nearer to basic church membership than organizing an adult devotional society at the church. We found these contrasting degrees of engagement in the study.

Another dimension of engagement is the sheer amount of time and the number of activities in which the respondents engaged. Contrast the young woman who was a member of the church youth group with the woman who belonged to two groups in the church, one of which was a social action group, and who also taught catechism.

At a different level of successful engagement were the young people who had leadership positions beyond the local membership organization. One young man was the president of the association of secondary school students for the state of Rio de Janeiro, and another was the first secretary of the Brazilian Union of High School Students. A third young man was treasurer of the same organization. Of the four young people who achieved leadership status in state and federal student organizations, two were from low-income and two from middle-income families.

Another aspect of the intensity of their engagement was shown by the passion with which the young people described their history of participation. Nine young people in our sample had remarkable trajectories of engagement and great conviction about their roles as young activists. Five of those had started their leadership careers as restless children who were elected by their classmates to represent them in negotiating with adults to defend their interests. Raquel (F/15) remembered taking a leadership role at a much younger age:

> My first memories of a leadership role were very simple, at age 9, when I was elected for the first time class representative. This work turned out well as shown by the fact that I stayed class representative for five years.

These young people recognized the intensity of their commitment to change:

> I've always been someone who questions things. I've always looked at things in this way and perceived things in a critical way. (Jonas, M/20)

> I've done various things, always seeking change; always having inside me a wish to change things. (Mateus, M/24)

This initiation into leadership positions is interesting in an age when school discipline has become such a big concern for teachers, principals, and parents. As mentioned before, several of these youths told us that they had been labeled restless and *bagunceiros* (naughty). They reported getting into trouble and even being expelled from school. Jessica (F/18) said:

> I've been stopped from organizing a school council in my school. When I wanted to do this, there were a series of accusations [made against the school]; I made one, and the administration ended up expelling me from school.

Her comment is a reminder of the challenges of disciplining children without suppressing their creativity and leadership skills, particularly when they ask the adults to think and behave differently.

The following section summarizes the *what* and the *how* of engagement. We examine the ways in which our group of young people saw Brazilian youths in general and the ways in which they thought about their own participation.

Envisioning: Their Political Ideas

In this section we discuss our respondents' ideas about young people's participation in society and about being their age, along with their views of the world. They had much to say about the common images of their generation, about how young people were regarded as being disengaged, politically unaware, indifferent, passive, or pessimistic:

> I guess that young people today, in general, are lifeless, very complacent. People don't see as much the *caras pintadas* getting out into the streets, protesting, making demands, speaking out loud; we don't see much of that.[7] (Talita, F/18)

> So I guess that, nowadays, young people are very tired, very complacent. They are politicized, but they think things aren't going to happen, and are pessimistic and don't fight for them. (Raquel, F/15)

Several youths in our study spoke about a disappointing lack of political concern from their peers (this came up particularly from those involved in political parties). Jonas (M/20) talked critically about a lack of political awareness, saying the young were concerned about themselves and the present:

> I am going to say something obvious. Young people today are alienated about political issues. You start talking to someone [about politics] and they say, "This is a drag"; "This doesn't interest me"; "I am not going to change anything." What is a person to think today? So, I am going out tonight, and am going to a nightclub, I am going to have fun.

Leonardo (M/24), a gay activist, mentioned his struggles to engage others:

> This question of youth not engaging in politics, I think, it's not just among the gay, but all young people in general don't have the patience for politics, and I see this when I desperately try to bring my friends, and the result is zero.

There are, of course, several reasons why young people have little faith in politicians. These reasons emerge in a number of studies. Evidence from the study "Brazilian Adolescents and Youth: Social and Political Participation" (UNICEF 2007) shows that while young people "favor" the idea of voting, they are divided about other forms of involvement. Some think that further participation is a good idea (55 percent), while others think that it should be avoided (41 percent).

Fifty-two percent of the young people interviewed for the UNICEF study thought that getting involved in politics changed them for the better, while 44 percent thought that political engagement made them worse, and 47 percent thought that politics was a contaminated arena. For this reason they believed that young people should look for other ways of participation (UNICEF 2007, 19).

Our respondents saw other reasons for disengagement. One was the fear and anxiety about the dangerous world around them. The current generation of young people feels exposed and vulnerable. Joana (F/17) said:

Young people today have had, how can I put it, very fast moving lives, and it is as if they have seen suffering and violence close up.

Mateus (M/24), a leader in the Landless Workers Movement, said:

Today, young people are much more directly affected. Every year many young people die as victims of daily urban warfare caused by a [general] state of violence and by social inequality.

Fernando (M/24), a young artist and activist, spent the first sixteen years of his life in a poor community that became extremely violent under the control of drug dealers. He commented on the daily realities there:

The young people who live in this community face many difficulties. First, they are in school and suddenly they can't go home because of a fight between a gang and the police, bringing shooting throughout the community. And so it's very complicated. You do not know if they can get used to this [situation]. In fact, you go to school and don't know if you are going to return, or if you are going to be able to go to school next day. (M/24)

It might be hard for people in less dangerous cities to comprehend the way in which violence overshadows daily life in Rio, particularly in poor communities, where the presence of violence is constant. According to the study *The Young People of Rio: Paths, Beliefs and Approaches* (Novaes and Mello 2002), Rio youths feel vulnerable to violence. More than 40 percent believe they could be the victims of violence, and 31 percent believe they could be hit by a stray bullet. Also notable is the number of young people who believe they are vulnerable to rape (10 percent) and traffic accidents (9.9 percent). Police violence appeared in 6.5 percent of our accounts. The relationship between violence and civic engagement is straightforward: Any out-of-the-ordinary activity in a community run by drug traffickers that brings a person to their attention puts that person at risk of physical harm and even death. In *favelas*, where different gangs (*commandos*) are struggling for dominance, there is also a risk from random gunfire as the gangs fight.

14. Protesting violence. Photo by Manuelle Rosa.

In addition to the fear of violence that can squelch any activist urges, our group of young people pointed out that there were other costs to civic engagement, chief among them the time that activism took up. Activism also took a toll on family life, because the activists lacked time to be with the family.

It's the absence, the absence, the absence 100 percent, isn't it? The absence for a long period of time from my family. It's a question of [even when] you are home, you come home more tired; you have an increased number of responsibilities [outside the home]. (Jessica, F/18)

My sisters complain many times about [my] absence, when can I take them to the beach, to the movies? Sometimes there is difficulty even in being with my boyfriend. (Talita, F/18)

And here's the problem, on the days they schedule all kinds of things, it is impossible for us to go [anywhere]. We do everything we can to go, but we can't because as we are leaving, Mom comes home and talks about one thing, then the stepfather comes home and talks about another thing, and you stay home with your head in the clouds. (Lucas, M/17)

The young people were also concerned about the time away from their studies, particularly when they were already trying to juggle education and work. As the statements below show, they simply could not keep up with all the demands, and sometimes their studies suffered:

Sometimes, I have to sacrifice a class. Sometimes that results in a bit of a low grade, and later I have to pull myself together in order to recuperate. (Leo, M/17)

I could be studying ten hours a day. Law school, you understand? I would like a career in law, too, and I am not able to do that because of the issue of my activism. But I don't regret that; I find it interesting. (Jonas, M/20)

If I did not take courses in the evenings, I would not participate in the party meetings; I would not go to Brasilia. To go to Brasilia, I had to miss the first day of class at school [laughs]. So every once in a while, when I have to travel, I miss going to English class, I miss going to morning class. (Raquel, F/15)

Not surprisingly, the young people also sacrificed leisure time to the demands of civic engagement.

So I prefer to give up my moments of leisure, of free time, to be in these places. So there is a sacrifice. (Leo, M/17)

Oh, I had to give up playing a lot; I did not have enough time to spend playing with my friends, to spend time going out, but these weren't things that I had to give up completely. (Marcia, F/16)

But many said the trade-offs involved in being engaged were worth it.

I stop being with my family, I stop doing other things, going to the beach, because I no longer have much time to do this work, but I don't regret it. It adds a lot to my life. (Jessica, F/18)

Why do they say that youth is the future of the nation? Youth is the present. (Raquel, F/15)

Finally, the possibilities of participation depend not only on the young people and their choices but also on the receiving institutions and organizations. Gabriel (M/23) said access was still limited for young people even in organizations where one would expect them to be welcome.

I think that the participation of youth is still very restricted. For example the Municipal Council of the Rights of Children and Adolescents—only various institutions participate in the assemblies; their administrative staff, their coordinating staff, and the youth are not there. (Gabriel, M/23)

Despite the challenges of participation, the tone of most interviews was one of hope. Even when the young people were talking about their disenchantment with people who did not seem to care about social issues, they were excited at the possibilities of being a young activist in a country where so many inequalities needed to be addressed. For Mateus (M/24), the challenge of changing society was the new faith, the new religion:

I have faith today in the social struggles, in the transformation of society. I do not know if it is faith. I believe that it is fundamental for the transformation of human beings. It's the struggle, it's the organization of the people, to give political direction for action through the struggles of the masses. Through an organization of the masses, we will have the transformation of society and with that we will have a better life, more justice, equality; so I believe that.

Moreover, the challenges of their current civic activities left these young people eager for a life of continued engagement. As they looked to the future, they described the common dreams of finishing their education and forming their own families. But they also expected that they would continue to participate in civic activities.

Well, I don't know what I will be doing, neither tomorrow nor ten years from now. . . . Today I am in high school, later university, suddenly I graduate. . . . I want to do journalism; I find this profession very attractive. And independent of where I will be, I think that the important thing is to participate, to be organizing. Whatever the category, whether it be in a union, or in a university. (Jessica, F/18)

Not to leave off fighting for the cause, but to be acting in these places, that's the way I see. So one of the things that I said to the participants in the congress [for children's rights] was that today you are the ones who are here; tomorrow it will be us. So it is a responsibility because if one day I make it there, and have that right to judge and to decide, having all that training is a much greater responsibility. (Leo, M/17)

We end this section with the major topics that propelled many of our young people into civic engagement and the concerns that continued to exercise them: the poor state of education in the country and its consequences, and the rights of political participation. We note that the young people are aware of the responsibilities that come with their demands and their rights, and we conclude with their views on responsibility.

Access to Education

Education was the issue most mentioned by the youths. They were concerned that the poor quality of education affects the capacity of young people to play their proper role in society and is a major source of inequality.

I think that education is the cradle of everything, so if you have a good education, certainly you will start to think differently; you will begin to create a different country; you begin to change. So you begin to create new youth and later adults with a different consciousness; I think that education will bring that to our country. (Denise, F/16)

I think that all of the problems that arise from social inequality, the inequality that you do not have a right to education, you do not have a right to food—that is where the violence comes from. (Raquel, F/15)

While some of the young people expressed their views about education as a right, others stressed the importance of education for facing the demands of the workplace.

The right to study, the right to graduate, if you want to graduate; I think that is important in the profession that you choose. The right to work, right? (Sabrina, F/18)

Freedom of Political Participation

While the young people saw education as the basis for a successful work life, they saw political participation as the force from which other important goals followed.

> Political participation is the main thing. Because everything else depends on political influence, all types of participation, sports, religion, the ability to change or not, the ability to exist or not, you understand? Politics is in everything and we, the youth, need to participate politically. (Jonas, M/20)

> It's the struggle; it's the organization of the people, to give political direction to the actions through the fights of the masses. Through an organization of the masses we will have the transformation of society, and with that, we will have a better life, more justice, equality. So I believe in that. (Mateus, M/24)

Becoming politically aware was important even if one disliked the processes of politics. This point was illustrated by Raquel (F/15):

> I hate politics in particular. But it was there that I began to perceive that sometimes it is not necessary to like something, but it is necessary to know a little bit, it is necessary to somewhat enter that politic itself, however much it may disturb you. It is important that we experience it to know about it, a little about things, of what politics is, and even more in a country like ours.

Responsibilities

Discussions of rights raise the parallel issue of responsibilities. It is noteworthy that this group of young activists drew a clear distinction between the responsibilities of childhood and youth and the responsibilities of adulthood, despite that fact that they had taken on civic responsibilities early in their lives. There was time enough for full adult responsibility later in life. This is how Felipe (M/19) expressed that point:

> In terms of responsibility, we tend to think that youth, at least, have fewer responsibilities, at least in the short term, right? In general the responsibilities would at least be less, but responsibilities are formed in youth; I think that is how they begin to be constructed.

And he added,

> First, it is a process in which you stop being a child, but also you are not yet an adult, and people begin to demand things from you.

Luciano (M/20) said:

> A young person is still in formation, right? He does not yet have a clear notion of responsibility. I see responsibility as discussing things, discussing, discussing, to put your head working, you know?

The primary responsibility young people had, they said, was to study to prepare for the future and then figure out how to get into the job market.

> Responsibility? Primarily school. I am beginning to realize that school is the fundamental thing; without it, we are nothing. I began to realize that because how am I going to get a decent job? These days, it is really hard to get a job even if you graduate from college. So I think the major responsibility is school, to get good grades, to study. (Leo, M/17)

> First of all study, study, study, study. Finish studying, give thanks to God. Then start the struggle for a job, because work is very difficult, the whole world is seeing that. (Lucas, M/17)

But the purpose of education was also to get a handle on the state of the world. What follows is the point of view of Mateus (M/24), the young activist in the Landless Workers' Movement.

> The task of youth today is, in fact, to study, to understand the Brazilian reality and the reality of Latin America and of the world, and, with that, to contribute to the social environment.

Being responsible is no light thing. Sometimes, the pressures are heavy. Some see that in fundamental terms:

> Ah, the responsibility with society, right? We have to give continuity to generations, so that is the responsibility. Here more youth are dying, right? With this violence, what will tomorrow be like? So we have to provide continuity for our generation and respect the generations that are coming. (Alexandra, F/17)

In contrast to the young people who thought that youth should not yet be asked to shoulder responsibilities as if they were adults, Raquel (F/15) insisted:

I think that one has responsibility because one is no longer a child. I think you have the responsibility to fight for what you want. You can't spend your whole life making excuses: "Ah, I didn't have a good school, I didn't have a good family, that is why I did not succeed." No, you did not succeed because you did not make the effort. When you are young, you are already mature enough to set your path.

Our respondents' notions of responsibility were, therefore, quite nuanced. While they saw their own activism in the light of their responsibilities to improve the world around them, they were clear that the primary responsibility of young people was to acquire an education and prepare for adult life. They also recognized that they must prepare for adult responsibilities and that, at the very least, they should be held accountable for their actions.

A Closing Comment

In practice, the inspiration for our young people to become civically active came from youth and other community-based organizations, and from the encouragement of friends and family. It also came from a strong sense of the difficulties and dangers facing young people in urban Brazil. The combination of the recent history of Brazil, its emergence from dictatorship, and the current levels of economic inequality and urban violence persuaded some young people to become engaged in society-changing ventures.

While some of the young people in Rio graduated to state and national positions, the occasions for engagement were, for the most part, local to their respective communities. So a precondition for engagement is the presence of such opportunities. While the common institutions of youth—church and school—can encourage or discourage youthful participation, they were for many of our respondents the staging grounds for their engagement. The small organizations that actively recruited young people for a variety of purposes provided the starting point for some of our respondents. Families were a complex influence; some were supportive, some discouraging, and some ambivalent. Some young people just fought their way into engagement out of impulses that came from deep within themselves.

We would need extensive surveys of youth participation in different countries to assess how Brazilian young people who are civically engaged are similar to or different from their counterparts elsewhere. But based on the general surveys described earlier, and on our sample, we do find in Brazil a strong sense of the importance of engaging in communal and cooperative activity for the good of the whole, in contrast to simply engaging for one's own benefit. It may well be that Brazil's recent history and the challenges facing the country have produced a stronger sense of the importance of cooperative and collective action than elsewhere.

Notes

Part of the research done by Irene Rizzini for this chapter was carried out thanks to the Helen Kellogg Institute for International Studies at the University of Notre Dame when she held a visiting chair in Brazilian Cultural Studies. The authors are grateful to the CIESPI research team that worked with them in this project: Paula Caldeira, Alessandra Caldeira, and Denise Barros. Other collaborators were Udi Mandel Butler and Marcelo Princeswal.

1. IBGE (Brazilian Institute of Geography and Statistics). The National Household Survey (PNAD)for the Rio metro area between 1993 and 2003adapted by the Data Resource on Children and Youth at the International Center for Research and Policy on Childhood, Rio de Janeiro, www.ciespi.org.br.

2. For this study, the researchers constructed a probability sample of the population of young people between the ages of fifteen and twenty-nine in Brazil, using as a base data from the Demographic Census of 2000 and the National Study of Household Samples (PNAD) of 2002.

3. The title of the book, chosen by the group, is *Nós: A Revolução de Cada Dia* (*We/Knots: The Revolution of Each Day*), 2007.

4. Brazil's Landless Rural Workers Movement is the largest social movement in Latin America, with an estimated 1.5 million members organized in twenty-three of the twenty-seven states. The goal of the MST is land reform in a country characterized by inequitable land distribution.

5. Mother Queen is part of one title of Mary, the mother of Jesus, and here refers to a church devotional group. This girl decided to volunteer to coordinate the Novena for Mãe Rainha (nine days of public or private devotion), in which the statute of Mary circulates from house to house and ends up in the girl's house.

6. Leonel Brizola was a charismatic Brazilian politician, the president of the PSDB (Partido da Social Democracia Brasileira) a national party, and a controversial populist governor of Rio de Janeiro.

7. The *caras pintadas*, or "painted faces," were the young people who demonstrated for the impeachment of the corrupt Brazilian president Collor de Mello in 1992.

References

Abreu, Alzira Alves de. 2000. "A imprensa e o engajamento político no final do século XX." Paper presented at XXIV Encontro Anual da ANPOCS, Petrópolis, 23–27 October. Retrieved from http://bibliotecavirtual.clacso.org.ar/ar/libros/anpocs00/gt08/00gt0813.doc.
Bordenave, Juan E. D. 2002. *O que é participação?* 8th ed. São Paulo: Brasiliense.
Brazil. 1988. *Constituição Federal* [Brazilian Constitution]. Brasilia.

Bush, Malcolm. 2008. *Barriers to Youth Connections to Work: The Case of Young People in the Low-Income Neighborhood of Caju in Rio de Janeiro*. Chicago: Woodstock Institute.

Butler, Udi, Marcelo Princeswal, and Roberta Silva. 2007. "Cultures of Participation." Rio de Janeiro: International Center for Research and Policy on Childhood (CIESPI).

IBASE and Instituto Pólis. 2005. *Juventude Brasileira e democracia: Participação, esferas e políticas públicas*. Rio de Janeiro: IBASE.

ISER (Instituto de Estudos da Religião). 2002. *Jovens do Rio: Circuitos, crenças e acessos*. Edited by Regina Novaes and Cecília Campello Mello. Rio de Janeiro: Comunicações do ISER, no. 57.

Krischke, Paulo J. 2004. "Perfil da juventude Brasileira: Questões sobre cultura política e participação democrática." *Revista Internacional Interdisciplinar INTERthesis* 1, no. 2. Santa Catarina: Programa de Pós-Graduação Interdisciplinar em Ciências Humanas, Universidade Federal de Santa Catarina (PPGICH UFSC).

Novaes, Regina, and Cecília Campello Mello, eds. 2002. *Jovens do Rio: Circuitos, crenças e acessos*. Rio de Janeiro: Comunicações do ISER 57, no. 2.

ONU (United Nations). 2003. *Relatório do Fundo de População das Nações Unidas: Situação da População Mundial*. New York: United Nations.

Renno, Lucio R. 2003. "Estruturas de oportunidade política e engajamento em organizações da sociedade civil: Um estudo comparado sobre a América Latina." *Revista de Sociologia e Política* 21 (November).

RITLA (Rede de Informação Tecnológica Latino-Americana). 2008. *Mapa da Violência: Os Jovens da América Latina*. Brasília: RITLA.

Rizzini, Irene, ed. 2010. *Direitos Humanos de Crianças e Adolescentes: 20 Anos do Estatuto*. Brasília: Secretaria de Direitos Humanos (Federal Secretariat for Human Rights).

Rizzini, Irene, and Gary Barker. 2002. "Promises Kept, Promises Broken: Recent Political and Economic Trends Affecting Children and Youth in Brazil." In *Globalization and Children: Exploring Potentials for Enhancing Opportunities in the Lives of Children and Youth*, edited by Natalie H. Kaufman and Irene Rizzini, 129–50. New York: Kluwer Academic/Plenum.

Statute of the Child and the Adolescent. 1990. Brazil. Law no. 8.069.

UNESCO. 2006. *Pesquisa Juventude, Juventudes: O que une e o que separa?* Brasília: UNESCO. Abramovay, Miriam and, Mary Garcia Castro, eds. Retrieved from http://www.unesco.org.br/publicacoes/livros/juventudesjuventude/mostra_documento. Retrieved from http://www.unesco.org/new/pt/brasilia/about-this-office/unesco-resources-in-brazil/studies-and-evaluations/violence/youth-in-brazil/.

UNICEF. 2007. *Adolescentes e jovens do Brasil: Participação social e política*. São Paulo: UNICEF, Instituto Ayrton Senna, and Itaú Social. Retrieved from http://www.unicef.org/brazil/pt/voz2007.pdf.

FOUR

New Paradigms of Civic Participation among Youth
A Study in Mexico City

Norma Del Río

Mexico may still be thought of as a country of young people, with more than half of its population under the age of thirty and one-third between twelve and twenty-nine years.[1] With abundant resources—it has the thirteenth-largest world economy, based on gross domestic product (World Bank 2011) —Mexico nevertheless has one of the highest rates of inequalities in the region, with a Gini index of .49 (OECD 2011). Although compensatory policies have been implemented to reduce poverty levels, inequality and exclusion continue to affect women and youth in particular. Among adolescents (ten- to seventeen-year-olds), one of every five males and one of every ten females are forced to work to earn a living (STPS-INEGI 2010).

The national elections of 2000 were considered a watershed for the country's "democratic transition," bringing to an end the seven-decade rule of the Institutional Revolutionary Party (PRI). But since the presidential elections of 2006, Mexico has been immersed in an institutional crisis, in which the credibility and the legitimacy of the electoral system have been seriously called into question. The degree of violence perpetrated by organized crime (including drug and human trafficking) has risen to the point that security has become a priority in the political agenda.[2]

The larger metropolitan area surrounding Mexico City produces one-third of the national gross domestic product (GDP) and has a population of about twenty million. The Federal District (DF) is the heart of the economic, political, social, and cultural life. Its nearly nine million inhabitants (of whom 25 percent are under the age of eighteen) have a per capita GDP that is 145 percent higher than the country's average; they also have one of Mexico's highest values on the Human Development Index (HDI), at .88 (INEGI 2005). However, a recent assessment on the status of human rights in Mexico City highlights the large differences that underlie that data, saying that the DF "is also among the 10 states that contribute most to national inequality" (DF 2008, 65).

In recent years, international human rights organizations have spoken to the need for participative democratic change in Mexico City. Following their recommendations, and under pressure from civil society, the DF's left-wing administration has enacted a series of laws, including the Federal District Act for the Rights of Boys, Girls and Adolescents in 2000. This law led to the creation of a Council for the Promotion of Children's Rights and mandates that spaces be provided for the participation of young people in public affairs (Articles 43 and 44). The Act for the Federal District's Youth was also enacted in 2000; it defines adolescents as legal beings (capable of rights and duties) and strategic social actors for the city's transformation and enhancement. The law defines youth as being fourteen to twenty-eight years old but distinguishes adolescents as minors, from fourteen to eighteen years of age. Articles 39 and 40 establish their right to organize and to obtain social recognition.

Another two laws complement the legal context for young people in Mexico City. A law to foster citizen participation, enacted in 2004, determines eleven possible forms of engagement and representation for city residents; the act for the prevention and eradication of discrimination, enacted in 2006, defines thirty-seven types of discriminatory practices through action or omission. However, there is still a gap between the legal sphere and the implementation of social policies that manage and provide democratic spaces for the real practice of citizenship.

> In Mexico, the democratic management of local youth policies is still pending. The legacy of a central state that promotes policies with a universal and sectorial focus, the diversity of young actors with little degree of coordination and the increasing social exclusion to which they are subjected, are some of the factors that limit the possibility to design and implement the new policies. (Domínguez Pérez and Gil De La Torre 2003).

Mexico's social policies have been developed with a lack of citizen participation in planning and decision making and have been organized by *corporativismo* (collective compulsory membership in the party in power through the main labor union).

Important changes have taken place recently as a result of the end of the one-party rule and of the work of a citizens' organization created to monitor elections. However, in Mexico, political participation is still often controlled by local political bosses who provide preferential treatment to a particular interest group in exchange for its political support (Durand Ponte 2004). This controls and distorts the forms of participation and explains the lack of engagement by Mexican youth in politics and their high degree of mistrust in institutions.[3] In a survey taken in 2005, only 1.5 percent of youth said they were actively involved in a political organization (IMJ 2006). And 76 percent of those interviewed in the 2000 National Youth Survey said their lack of interest was a reaction to government corruption and the perception that private interests interfere and undermine the public interest (Flores 2003). And indeed, political parties insert themselves in schools, co-opting and recruiting youth to enlarge their ranks, to create "clash groups," popularly known as *porrismo*, and to organize "vote baskets" (prefilled polls). This has weakened the legitimacy and tarnished the image of student organizations in the promotion and leadership of social change (Castillo Berthier 1996). Much remains to be done before the definition of youth as strategic actors can, in real practice, become a differentiated policy.

The Participants

Of the thirty organizations we contacted, ten from civil society and one from the government responded that young people, ages ten to twenty, were active members in their projects. From those groups, twenty-two young people (eleven women and eleven men) were willing to participate; they were between the ages of twelve and twenty-four, with an average age of seventeen; they came from different socioeconomic levels and different parts of the city. Of the twenty-two, ten lived in highly impoverished areas, four lived in residential areas, and the others came from low-income neighborhoods. Veronica (F/18), a Greenpeace volunteer, explained:

> I really like my house. That is, I cannot go out and run in the streets because there is nowhere for me to do so. There is nothing but pavement and just a little bit of grass. There are no parks close by, either. It's not like there is a huge space out there. It is the city.

As in Rio de Janeiro and Chicago, social cohesion has been eroding in Mexico City due to residential, school, and social segregation.[4] The fact that Mexico City is one of the largest metropolises in the world makes civic participation even more difficult. Most young people have to invest a great deal of their free time in traveling to school or to the organizations in which they are active, often at the other end of the city. Insecurity, which has been declared a national problem, limits the community interaction of many young people, especially of women: "The truth is, we do not get along with people in our neighborhood. I only talk to my next-door neighbor and one who lives at the corner," said Graciela (F/18), another Greenpeace volunteer who lives on the outskirts of town.

The youngest of our participants, Nora (F/13), whose family was left homeless by the 1985 earthquake, explained: "I don't see [friends and neighbors] much because of the insecurity. [My parents] don't let me go out much. Maybe I get in touch by phone or the Internet, but not a lot."

Even though the laws guarantee freedom of association, young boys tend to be a control target because of their appearance. Alejandro (M/16), who had been participating in a media project (Ixtehuan) since he was fourteen years old, attested to this: "Although we may think we are simply hanging out with friends, and we're going to play soccer, if someone else sees us, they're either afraid or believe we're a gang."

Some of the young people complained that they are often victims of stereotypes: "I think the problem is that before seeing why they could be friends with someone, instead they look for a reason to turn them into their enemy. If you try to behave really well, then you're *fresa*.[5] If you look rather harmless, then they come after you," said Enrique (M/15), a participant in Machincuepa, a social circus project, who has found it difficult to settle into his new neighborhood, located only a few blocks from where he previously lived.

Still, most of the low income youth interviewed had family relationships that formed a protective network: "Here nearly all families have some sort of connection: There is always someone who is either another person's godfather, uncle, or neighbor," Enrique added. The researcher Larissa Lomnitz (1975) has described these solidarity networks in the city's squatter settlements where many of these young people lived.

The participants in our study still lived at home with their families, more than half of them in traditional nuclear structures. Their parents held a variety of jobs. Although the mother was a central figure who provided some sort of structure and was close to them, the presence of grandmothers and other relatives in the house was common among one-third of the young people; the father held a marginal place and was absent in two-thirds of the cases. These figures agree with the results of a youth survey carried out in Mexico in 2006 (IMJ).

Migration had played an essential role in family dynamics: one-third of the families of the young people were headed by the mother,[6] and the same proportion of fathers and relatives had migrated to another part of Mexico or to another country. One of our subjects of indigenous origin, Miriam (F/16), a promoter of Children Rights in Cuauhtémoc Municipality, migrated to the city when she was eight to live with her parents, who had migrated when she was a baby.

Description of Organizations

The participants in our study belonged to eleven organizations that focus on a variety of social concerns, from environmental issues to family planning and children's rights. Following Pittman's classification of youth engagement projects, we found that only three organizations had objectives that were more developmental and preventive (youth as service recipients) in relation to youth participation, while the others were geared toward civic engagement, youth leadership, and organizational skills in the promotion of social change (Pittman, Martin, and Williams 2007).

Participation in the organizations enabled the young people to become familiar with a variety of topics and to develop skills (Bartko 2005); moreover, it provided them with the opportunities to reflect on citizenship issues (rights, diversity, gender, communal interests) and to reach their own conclusions. The motivational component of civic engagement was fulfilled through community activities. The opportunity for bonding and connecting with others developed their sense of collective identity, and their creative and innovative participation in the public sphere had strong implications for revitalizing the notion of citizenship and political participation (Flanagan, 2003). We remark on these processes in greater detail in the following sections, in which we describe the characteristics of the civic engagement of the young people.

Youth's Educational and Labor Trajectories

Even though 90 percent of our interviewees were in the fifteen- to nineteen-year-old age group in which educational exclusion affects 32 percent of youth in Mexico City (it increases to nearly half at the age of nineteen) (Ulloa Herrero and Ulloa Pizarro 2006), we found discontinuities in school trajectories in only four cases. Two of them followed what Machado Pais (2000) described as the "yo-yo trajectory"; this refers to the patterns seen among youth who come and go from one situation to another—from student to worker, for example. That was the case of Miriam (F/16), the indigenous girl who, after two years of helping out at the family's street stand, was finally able to take the admission exam for *bachillerato* (the equivalent of a high school senior); her father had prevented her from taking the exam three years earlier. Antonio (M/23), one of our older participants, also had this type of trajectory. He suspended his university studies to establish and consolidate the social organization he now leads (Tepocatl) and then went back to school two years later, at the time when we interviewed him.

These young people from impoverished areas have had to evaluate the costs of remaining in a linear educational trajectory (De Ibarrola 2005). Enrique (M/16) reflected:

> People who study don't have a job, while often those who do not study find one more easily, so it is somewhat traumatic to think about.[7] However, I'd rather keep on studying; somehow, one day I'll have an opportunity.

Those who study youth labor in Mexico agree that the number of labor hours (more than twenty hours a week) competes with the opportunity to study (Knaul 2002), which means that young people depend on their family's support to continue studying. In three of our cases, individuals were under pressure to decide whether to stop studying at the end of their *bachillerato* or to go on to university; to continue with their own projects, they negotiated with their parents (Machado Pais 2000).

"When I told them I wanted to study philosophy, they were all surprised. They were afraid. 'You're going to go hungry. That doesn't pay. What is that? What do you want?' But now they've seen how I've developed . . . How they see me now, it's different. It's interesting," said Juan (M/24), who comes from a large, single-parent family whose mother did not go beyond grade school.

In our study, we found diversity in personal characteristics—some were extroverts, others had a taste for solitude and internal reflection. Their love of reading and their having acquired different communication skills—whether in video, radio, film, or simply the written word—were manifestations of a wide range of interests. This is clear from the statements of four respondents, all living in highly impoverished areas:

I was searching. I took workshops in painting, guitar, theater. (Juan, M/24, an active member in two projects, Machincuepa and Ixtehuan)

I have always been very hyperactive, very restless. I don't like staying quiet, I like to be doing many things. (Jimena, F/16, also from the Machincuepa Circus Project)

I want to study, finish school, and go on to university. I do want to study. (Karen, F/16, from the Ixtehuan video project)

What interests me the most is to learn. Whatever I do, I will do on my own, for myself. (Enrique, M/16 from Machincuepa)

Despite being economically dependent on their families, these young people had managed to build a sense of autonomy and competence. They were fully aware of the different social statuses that existed in Mexico: "I feel extremely thankful for life," said Verónica (F/18), a Greenpeace activist who hails from an upper-middle-class family. Basilio (M/18) recognized the exclusion and discrimination in the "elite" school environment that he had attended and looked for a more "humanist" school. Verónica and Basilio affirmed, with self-assurance, that success in life would be solely up to them.[8]

I am the kind of person who wants to do everything. The truth is, I want to eat [take on] the world; these dreams can be turned into reality. What prevents me from doing what I want to do to help myself, and not only me, but the people around me? At least, that's how I see it. OK, so what, in your opinion, are my limits? There are no limits; the truth is that there are no limits. You set the limits. You can go as far as you want. (Graciela, F/18)

This was in contrast with those whose encounters with discrimination and inequality had set the limits for their self-fulfillment. Note the observations made by Susana (F/20), an activist with a motor disability and the founder of SeLíder, and Javier (M/18) a participant of Machincuepa since he was 13.

You have to know when to be a perfectionist, and when not to be one. You have to know how far you can go as a human being: When it is good to wear makeup or not. When you've given it all you've got, it's not a matter of always being superheroes. I like the way I am, being natural, to give of myself. If you're not very pretty or handsome, too bad, that's the way life is. (Susana, F/20)

I do like to set challenges for myself, but I don't expect miracles. (Javier, M/18)

Coherence in Youth's Social Identity Building

The way the young people described themselves revealed confidence and determination to carry out their projects, although their ability to act depended on the place they held in society:

I am the sort of person that, when I want something, I try to get it, and I do. In life you must do what you believe in, see what you feel, and say it, so I try to do that all the time. . . . I'm not the type of person who cares what others think. (Julia, F/17)

We are like little elves all over the place. We try to do as much as we can. It is a fact. You can do it. It's hard; it is hard, and at times as students, we have a real hard time. (Antonio, M/23)

Although most of our subjects were Catholic, several were critical of religion, pointing out the distinction between their faith and the institution (the church); others talked about their interest in Buddhism, Protestantism, and Judaism, and one young girl confessed to believing in the vengeful power of the Saintly Death"—a popular cult figure, condemned by the Catholic church—who has a large following among "darkettos."[9] Some of the young people expressed a belief in a higher power, or in humanism, without adopting any particular religion; for others, religion was considered a limitation, something that people who felt insecure resort to as a refuge. "Personally I have strong beliefs, but in mankind. . . . That is, I believe a human being has the ability both to do things and undo them. . . . [Many people] don't do something because the Bible says do not do this, or because they were told God would not want them to do something," Graciela (F/18) said.

Religion was frequently associated with political power—both of which were perceived to operate under a double standard—and seen as a manipulative force. An activist in the fight for sexual rights, Fernando (M/17) considered: "We have an ultra right-wing culture in which our cardinal wants to get involved in politics."

Another social activist, Antonio (M/23), argued:

We should maintain the schools' lay status, as well as freedom of religion. It's good that our country was a pioneer on this issue, because there are

still many countries that do not separate church and state. Many continue
to have parties that are Catholic or of other religions. Religion provokes
a lot of division among people. . . . There are difficult historical contexts
that are closely linked to politics. Unfortunately, religions take advantage
of people's needs to fool and enrich themselves.

Miriam (F/16), the young indigenous woman, and Juan (M/24), a resident
of a poor neighborhood, spoke of the imposition of religion as a symbol
of the conquest during the colonial period. She talked about the personal
conflict she had had in trying to integrate religion with a part of her identity;
he was thinking of studying theology.

We found that the young people interviewed shared a sense of ethics
and morals that on occasion may be identified with spirituality.

> I understood that maybe you don't have a problem with doing something,
> but that others may be hurt by your actions. Values are like a law that
> rules over us, this path I'm talking about, in which you share and talk
> with others amicably, regardless of each individual's beliefs . . . but yes,
> I do know there has to be a social order. (Alejandro, M/16)

> To love your neighbor and love thyself and love others, to take care of
> them and not do them harm and all that; then, based on these values—
> universal ones, not of any particular religion—to be able to respect others
> and to take them into account. (Horacio, M/19)

> It has something to do with your spirit; you are somehow purified when
> trying to help someone achieve a particular aim. (Verónica, F/18)

Civic engagement put the young people in a position where they could listen, observe, and empathize. This made them willing not only to help but
also to relate "in a feast of understanding," as Verónica (F/18) said. Other
respondents agreed:

> To know how to encourage others, to have empathy on occasion, to put
> yourself in the other's shoes. . . . Then I like to observe the person, put
> myself in his/her mind somewhat, see what is happening to them, what
> they are thinking. (Antonio, M/23)

> I like to relate to others. As I say, to learn from them and with the little
> bit that I have, they may learn from me. And for them to teach me the
> thoughts on life they may have; their other views on life. (Jimena (F/17)

A sense of social responsibility was a characteristic that we found in most of these young people, an element that rules their daily actions and distinguishes them from others of the same age. Verónica (F/18), Greenpeace activist, said:

> I don't do things just for the sake of doing them; rather, I think about the consequences of all my actions and what the repercussions may be for others. That is why I say that you really have to think carefully about what you do, in order not to hurt others, but on the contrary, to help them.

Miriam (F/16) saw this kind of sensibility as negative, since it expresses the need to depend on others and seek their approval. But others recognized it as part of their identity: "I think that is what sets me apart: the story of how I grew up. I really like to take care of people and make sure they are well; that those close to me are well, and also those who are not so close. How to achieve something good for all, that is what could distinguish me somewhat from my friends," said Horacio (M/19), a volunteer at Colonias de Vacaciones.

To be responsible for others is not merely an abstract issue; it is marked by the social roles traditionally assigned in Mexican culture as part of an individual's responsibilities. Several young women mentioned having to look after their siblings while their parents were at work; some of them became substitute mothers (this was the case of Miriam, an indigenous migrant), either because a sibling had migrated and left children behind, or due to the demands of an extended family, which meant that someone had to take care of nephews or cousins.

On Becoming Engaged: Early Influences, Links, and Social Awareness

Family

In this section we analyze the role that family played in the social participation of young people. One-third of the families supported and even looked for social activities for their children. The "protective" role so often mentioned in relation to community projects as safe spaces (Chaskin and Baker 2006; Halpern, Baker, and Mollard 2000) motivated several parents to support their children's engagement, especially in the case of young boys. Javier (M/18) writes in "My Experience in the Circus": "My mother didn't like me to be out in the street so much—the community we live in is not very nice—she was afraid something would happen to me. That is why she enrolled me in the circus" (Serrano Pineda 2007).

Other young people discussed with their parents the possibility of participating in an activity, negotiating the use of their free time. Karen (F/16), spoke about her discussions with her mother, who works full time as a peddler: "She wants me to be more productive or to spend my time on things that might be good for me." Five of the young people said their parents were distant and reserved. The rest of the families showed a certain resistance to the activism of their children.

The youths' committed participation had an ambivalent effect on this third group of parents. At first, the parents were resistant and fearful, particularly when they realized this was not simply a passing interest. The young people were forced to fight social stereotypes within their own families, finding themselves rejected and mocked, or seeing the social significance of their engagement put down. The parents' complaints were along the lines of, "You work too hard, you're doing too much and not getting anything in exchange," or "Son, you're taking on too much, why don't you just drop it?" Verónica (F/18) explained that in her well-to-do family being different was equal to being a rebel, hippie, or drug addict. The project's oldest participants, Juan and Antonio, who come from low-income neighborhoods, had this to say:

> [My mother] believes that these are just weird phases I'm going through. My sisters, too, see me as—I'm not sure—more rebellious. Not rebellious, but with another way of thinking, different from theirs. (Juan, M/24)

> "[My mother] has a son who is a troublemaker, an activist who likes to get involved in social issues, who gives talks and provides information on sexual health, who lets others know about condoms and all that. She very nearly had a heart attack!" (Antonio, M/23)

To retain their commitment to activism and be allowed to go about independently, some young women had to negotiate certain limits with their families. This issue did not come up with the young men, despite the fact that both men and women in the group said they had been held up for money.

To many families, the children's activism opened new ways of thinking. Topics that had been taboo were now out in the open, and parents responded positively when their children invite them to go somewhere. Fernando (M/17) talked about the changes his family has gone through:

It was little by little. First we touched on one topic, then another, then the most sensitive ones, such as sexual diversity. The thing was, how could you show up with a gay or lesbian friend? "Look mother, she's a lesbian, or she's a transvestite." Today, if I do that, it's no big deal. My mother even goes with me to gay places, to the protest marches and all that, and there's no problem. I have a twelve-year-old sister, and I don't know what kind of education she would have had if I had not changed. Now she gives talks in her school; my cousins now speak openly about all issues.

Alejandro (M/16) also began to see a new attitude at home:

Sometimes, I talk to my father; he says he is amazed because he's around forty years old, and he says, "I only realized this about five years ago, and in all my life, see what I've accomplished. It's not much, and you're only sixteen," and he seems surprised.

Juan (M/24) said that, because of his opinions, he gradually acquired a new position in his family and gained credibility and moral authority: "When an important decision must be made, or when something needs to be done, on occasions, I'm the one who's there."

School

None of our subjects said they were engaged in student organizations. After we posed the question directly, Enrique (M/16) told us that elections to represent the student body are perceived as populist and opportunistic:

They elect the representative according to the group's interests. Usually they choose someone who kind of goes along with everything, such as playing ball in the classroom, skipping classes, jotting down your attendance in class when you didn't go, or things like that. That's how they elect representatives.

For her part, Miriam (F/16), who moved to the city from the mountains of Guerrero, described a negative experience in elementary school. Often, she said, she skipped school and sought refuge in the nearby public library:

I came to Mexico City when I was like in third grade. The truth is, it feels really bad because nobody wants to have anything to do with you because you're indigenous; in grade school, I had no girlfriends and I had a real hard time understanding everything the teacher said. It was very hard for me, I was embarrassed to speak Spanish, my language was

Nahuatl. At school they made fun of me because I'm dark skinned, also because of the way I combed my hair and the way I spoke, I didn't know very well how to pronounce certain words. I remember that when I didn't understand something, the teacher would pull my hair. Sometimes I cried.

That is how Miriam described her time in grade school.

Only two young men who attended private Catholic schools mentioned social service. However, one out of every five mentioned a teacher whose teachings and careful listening left an imprint, or who suggested reading something meaningful and timely.

Social Organizations

Community work, staging demonstrations in different public places, the use of informative flyers and brochures, participation in public campaigns, and exhibits, as well as showing work in youth festivals, were important ways of youth participation as members of the social organizations, and at the same time they served to attract other young people. Another significant factor was a relationship with adults who were good listeners:

> It seems that I always tend to look for older people, maybe because they can teach me something. I don't know, maybe a book, or their experience in life and other things; it is easier for me to learn from them. (Camila, F/16)

Speaking about the relationship with other adult Greenpeace members, Julia (F/17) commented:

> We trust each other even though we may not know each other, because in a way our ideas are similar, so we know we can talk about anything we want, anything at all, right? And we're going to be with persons who will understand us.

Alejandro (M/16) recognized the valuable tutoring and understanding that Gustavo and Lalo (the adults in charge of Ixtehuan) gave him, as he began to make his own videos:

> Gustavo helped me a great deal. He told me how to edit my video, gave me some tips on how to put the music, edit and process the images; with Lalo we became good friends. Now he's in another workshop for adults, where they teach them to develop their imagination; he told me about some exercises in which you have to let your imagination run wild. I

think he's helped me to get along with others, to not be afraid of those who are older.

Young men and women told us repeatedly about the importance of being in a warm and open environment:

It has shown me to share and have a good time with others, to not be afraid of older people, like some friends of mine who are afraid or become inhibited if they have to talk with older people. (Alejandro, M/16)

I liked the way they addressed us as peers; there was trust, responsibility, and respect the way they spoke among them. (Fernando, M/17)

It opens up a whole new world; you realize you can make your own decisions. When you go there, people are there for you. (Lilia, F/15)

Juan (M/24) commented on the value of these places:

They let you be and develop. You go in, and it doesn't matter what you're like, you're accepted. They don't judge you; they don't say anything to you. They give you the chance to explore yourself. It's like getting to know yourself.

They talked about being in places where tolerance was practiced, and the degree of engagement that the young man or woman might be in at a given moment was respected.

The first day of our meetings as promoters, I didn't understand a great deal. I felt they spoke in a manner I didn't always understand. But I always went when they invited me to these meetings, although I didn't talk and only listened. I really liked them, because I knew I was learning little by little. At times I felt like speaking, but I felt so nervous that I didn't say anything. (Miriam, F/16)

The value of achieving social recognition when they acted in the public sphere was especially significant for youths who had been ignored by others and subjected to stigmatization and social discrimination. The chance to project their competencies and be acknowledged as an active member of the organization fulfilled their need to belong and developed an image of respect. Nestor (M/15), who was involved in the Social Circus Project, ended his narration with a proud reference to his recent accomplishment: "Mom, buy the book. I'm Nestor, I'm in a book" Enrique (M/16) said: "At times,

15. Collage of community circus activities, 2007. Photo by Jesus Pille Corona.

really cool things happen, like when they tell you, 'Hey, you are from the circus, I saw you in the circus'" (Morales Razo 2007).

Miriam (F/16), who participated in an after-school program for indigenous people, wrote about how she addressed the challenge posed by one of her tutors, which eventually led her to join the Council for the Promotion of Children's Rights:

> —Miriam, I want to know if you'd like to participate in a contest on the rights of boys and girls.
> Why did she ask me? I gave no signs of being intelligent. Besides, I was very shy and knew nothing about contests, but I ended up saying:
> —Yes, what do I have to do?
> And she replied:
> — Well, you can make a drawing or write something.
> —The fact is I can't draw very well, I'd rather write . . . but I've never written. But, yes, I'll do it. Besides, I'm not concerned about winning.
> . . . . A few days later, they told me my writing had won first place in my category. Wow! I couldn't believe it. I simply couldn't understand why I'd won.

Social Conscience

The chance to create new social networks and share experiences with their peers was an important incentive to engagement:

> There were teenagers who were restless, afraid, and curious about the same issues I was. And it was really nice, because we all had the same concerns and we grew and learned among ourselves, and then we taught other young people. (Fernando, M/17)

Another incentive was the chance to teach others, to lend a helping hand and feel part of the community (Clary and Snyder 1999): "I like working with children and thought it would be a good way to help," Horacio (M/19) said when describing his reasons for participating in "Colonias de Vacaciones." He added: "Colonias is a place where things are done lovingly, those who go there do things for others gladly, they give and receive love."

To this gaze toward the outside world, we can add a desire for change and advocacy and a vision of the future, which are present even among the youngest of our participants, together with a genuine concern about what happens in their surroundings. All of this points to their insertion in the time and place they were living in, and their awareness of it. Several young girls and women joined an ecological movement from a need to contribute something and to protect the environment in light of its deterioration. Julia (F/17) explained: "When I was twelve, out of the blue, I got this really strange feeling to protect the environment. I began to realize all this and felt like doing something, somehow, to have an influence on people or make them aware of why it is important, or at least why I care."

This impulse among young people to find solutions to problems they perceived was part what led many to activism. Some lamented that their enthusiasm was not shared by others in their generation. Verónica (F/18) expressed her surprise at her classmates' apathy: "Once a 'teacher' came from Canada and asked who had ever worked in an organization, or helped out someone.[10] Nobody raised his hand. I couldn't believe it. I felt, 'How can this be!'"

Alejandro (M/16) reflected on the prevalent political culture that transmits within the family a sense of impotence along with a perceived distance between the private and public life: "No matter what you do, it looks as if you don't have the power to decide on your own . . . we usually say: 'politics must stay apart from where we are' . . . we don't get in . . . they do what they want . . . the power is very far from the people . . . it is a circle . . . if parents don't educate their daughters and sons for the change, there is much damage done to the community and to ourselves . . . values are learned within the family . . . we have to go against the current and participate."

Antonio (M/23) argues on the same line of thought:

> There is much apathy on young people, but it has been generated by adults, call it government, parents, teachers. We have been accustomed to acknowledge that they have to do it all, that we must receive everything, to have things solved by others . . . so now they present youth as incapable, tiresome beings that can't do nothing but destroy, that our proposals are not good . . . this social pressure ends when they succeed to have us leave behind our dreams and feel we have failed . . . but in spite of this, I see stronger generations coming if they have enough information and opportunities.

Activism was specifically pointed to by two of the young people, although others spoke of social responsibility and the importance of defending children's visibility: "Children matter in this project," said Nora (F/13), the youngest participant in our group. Often, their engagement was rooted in critical experiences that provoked a big emotional shock and indignation. For Fernando (M/17), the impetus was the death of a close friend in a case of attempted rape; for Jimena (F/17), a visit to a relative in prison; for Miriam (F/16), the rejection by her father because she is a woman, something that made her leave home on several occasions; for Antonio (M/23), it was witnessing the sale of drugs in his high school.

> When I got to school Monday I found out she had been killed. It was really hard, it freaked me out totally, she was like my sister, we'd shared everything since grade school and that's when I said: "No, no, it can't be. It can't be that women are raped and beaten; that because they don't let themselves be raped they are murdered!"
>
> I still feel a lot of indignation. This also had a strong influence on my decision to work as an activist. To not just let things be. . . . (Fernando, M/17)

> My uncle is in jail. They sentenced him to fifteen years. When we go see him, many of the detainees tell us why they were imprisoned. And it's shocking; You're here because you stole a piece of pastry? And others are there because they committed murder, and yet they're out in three days. I think that's unfair, don't you? There is a lot of maliciousness inside. I say this is my ideal: to get out of prison those who have no reason to be there; to get them out. (Jimena, F/17)

> I did not want to go back to my parents, but I started to think about my sister, the youngest one. If this is how my father treats me now, always saying all women are the same, I then asked myself, who is going to help my little sister? (Miriam, F/16)

> I saw how drugs were introduced into the schools, the drug trafficking was obvious. Thank God I've never had a problem, but it's there, it affects you. They give drugs to a young girl or a young boy . . . these type of situations are truly unfortunate, so then you try to do something. (Antonio, M/23)

Engaging: Issues, Practices, and Space

For young people to decide to become socially or politically active means confronting the subordinate relationship of power and the adults' hypocrisy. Lucia (F/20) remarked:

> Businessmen themselves look down on us. They say. "They're kids." So we, who are trying to organize ourselves to foster that [youth participation and presence], we are the first to face that no one wants to help. It's really hard to break down barriers. You have to keep telling yourself, "Even if they don't help me, I'll manage."

Genaro (M/19), the producer of a radio program called *Among Young People*, had a similar realization when he tried to find work in the media:

> First, they want to make money. They have their own interests, and without money, especially without sponsors, there is no place for you in radio. We sought opportunities through the university, struggling, trying to see the right people, media celebrities and company executives, showing them the project. We printed around eighty projects for eighty people.

When young people initiate a project, they're often hard-pressed to find support. It's even harder when they have no social assistance networks and come from a poor socioeconomic background. While upper-middle-class Genaro took less than a year to formalize and accredit his organization (Causa Joven) without having to quit his studies, it took Antonio (M/23) more than twice as long to create Tepocatl, and as mentioned earlier, he had to quit school to work and finance the project. Antonio described the situations he had to face as he developed Tepocatl:

> "There is a problem, guys and gals. We want to continue to support you, but unfortunately those at the top of the political precinct are putting pressure for you to leave." . . . I felt they were afraid that someone like us, the young men and women who know what problems we are facing day-to-day, would come with new proposals, new ideas, and that at the end of the day, our project would be a much better one than the ones they had. . . . We had to go through loads of bureaucracy, fill out all sorts of requisitions, endless requisitions we were not familiar with, but even so we managed to do it.

However, the young people whose activism took place within already established organizations did not face those obstacles. The organizations enabled them to carry out their projects and gave them the necessary backup: from the conception and proposal, the systematizing of information, its execution and production, to the public presentation, for example, in their own forums, at youth documentary festivals, or at public events and political councils. With this help, the young people discovered they were creators and authors: "You've got ideas; maybe adults cannot imagine what you do, but I can," one young girl said. Camila (F/16) discovered her drawing skills, looked for animation workshops and other visual-arts places, and set up a book club in her community, following the guidance of a teacher from whom she sought advice.

Teamwork led the young people to acknowledge one another, no matter how different they might be, and to create links and make new friends, at times overcoming situations in which peers at first showed their prejudices.

> Some new people who came in had a lot of prejudices when they saw us, since we are a very diverse group. One would say: "What am I doing here with these filthy guys who are not doing anything?" . . . And then we began to relate; we began knowing each other, and this guy realized that is simply the way we look . . . now we even kid about it. But he has also gone through his own process and changed the way he is and thinks, within the group,"

said Juan, (M/24) who managed to merge the circus activities with a social script multimedia show. In this process, young people also discovered their competence as social leaders—not because they held the highest positions in the hierarchy, but because they had the capability to set up and guide a team based on the projects on which they wanted to work. Alejandro (M/16), for example, described the process of leading a film production team:

> The level of complexity this requires plus how I needed to organize myself and others . . . because, since they're my age we like to have fun. I had to take the initiative and organize them. I gradually realized all this.

Antonio (M/23) recalled how his Tepocatl team overcame the hurdles to formally establish the group, and said: "When we see the list of beneficiaries, and assess the results and goals we achieved, there are many more people now. How did we do it? We can't believe it. But yes, it can be done."

The participants described the development of their social competencies as a process of becoming aware and acquiring knowledge, which implied being socially accountable. They said that young people were often accused of being apathetic and indifferent, when they were simply not well informed or aware of the issues. They recognized the importance of producing videos, radio programs, material for outreach and dissemination, and of using the mass media to spread awareness and reach young people in their own language, from peer to peer, and using a variety of formats.[11] Fernando (M/17), the activist for sexual diversity rights, said:

> The youth committee provides the young people's vision to the entire organization. It creates material for the young. Not the typical comic book of the eighties that no one reads. We've made brochures, videos, radio

spots. We also have a radio program online. It's called Radio Rockola. It's for young people. We invite specialists on different topics, and since it's online, we like to think everyone listens to it.

Susana (F/20), a film student, stated:

That's practically what I do: communicate. Film is big, and secondly, it has an impact, more so than television or radio. In the media, on television, on film, I can transmit messages addressing the problems of the young, of human rights, of world violence. I can take them where they are most needed.

Engagement took place not only in the streets and in the communities, but also in virtual space. The Internet opened new ways for Juan (M/24) to maintain personal contacts with mates working in Brazil, and for Susana (F/20), who would otherwise have a hard time moving due to her physical disability, to coordinate her meetings and agenda. Karen, a participant in Ixtehuan, said: "Not all young people can be heard in their communities because they don't have the means. The few of us who are lucky to be here can provide that tool."

The young people learned about technology at the same time that they went through a process of reflection. Their participation in organizations that operated through highly structured social and cultural networks gave them the opportunity to explore a variety of topics and opened platforms rarely accessible to a young city person. Among other activities, the young people were able to offer the views of the poor on poverty through independent community radio, to create short films on HIV, to participate in a TV interview on the role of young disabled women, to publish a newspaper article featuring an interview with the general director of the National Commission for the Development of Indigenous Peoples, and to participate in a youth forum with presidential candidates.

Another advantage of working with established organizations was the opportunity they provided to enter the international arena. One-fourth of these young men and women were able to travel abroad to represent their organizations and to exchange experiences with others. Fernando (M/17) wrote about his work with the Mexfam Foundation:

The way the foundation believes and invests in you is incredible. That is where I have hooked up with other NGOs and agencies such as the United Nations Population Fund, where I participated in the creation of a committee for the projection of a youth perspective within the organization.

Travel also gave the young people an opportunity to contrast different political and social realities. That was again the experience of Fernando, who, as a result of his participation in a meeting sponsored by the Planned Parenthood Foundation in Washington, DC, learned about the limits in the access to HIV information that many U.S. youths still experience, and how El Salvador's repressive system could inhibit free expression of gay youth and could criminalize condom distribution campaigns:

> At least in Mexico, I can speak, I can express myself and give condoms. I have these liberties. People take on these enterprises in spite of difficulties. I have the space to do it, while other countries face more obstacles. Because of this, I am proud to be a Mexican.

For Miriam (F/16), her situation as an indigenous migrant ceased to be a stigma after she traveled, with UNICEF's support, to represent Mexico's indigenous children in Madrid. The new role legitimized her identity. Since then, she has assumed the mission of disseminating the declaration written by indigenous boys and girls from Latin America on the Rights of Indigenous Children and Adolescents (July 2005), "so you may help me and many other children to learn about our rights and make sure they are enforced." (Mendoza Ascencio 2007, 52). She has become well known for her denunciation of ethnic discrimination toward migrant indigenous children in the city and has been featured in national newspapers and in a Colombian portal entitled "Ethnic Current Events" (Bolaños Sánchez 2006).

Juan (M/24) explained how a trip had helped develop his social conscience: "My travel to Brazil aroused my Latin American conscience. We have the same problems and share the same vision."

Susana (F/19) is now part of UNICEF's advisory board, but her long trajectory has shown her how to convert a stigma into an exceptional challenge. Her disability led her to embark on a serious career of activism before she was twelve, always in the company of her mother, an architect. Susana's story may be found on the World's People Blog. Along with twelve other Mexican women, Susana was nominated for the Nobel Peace Prize. She has direct access to well-known figures in politics and the media, which has enabled her organization, named SeLíder ("Be a leader"), to establish a feasible agenda of youth activities. Susana knows how to handle herself as a public figure and to defend her privacy and recognize her limitations. Despite the effort and energy needed to be an active participant in several forums, she continues to study for a bachelor's degree in communications.

16. Participants working on their publication, 2006. Photo by Norma Del Río.

Envisioning: Their Political Ideas

As noted, we cannot talk about only one type of youth trajectory; we have to consider several, in accordance with the social realities of the individuals. Most social policies geared to the youth sector seem to be designed for at-risk youth (Butler and Abreu 2007) and respond to stereotypes reinforced by an increasingly segmented citizenship (San Juan, 2006). This paternalistic perception, which views citizens as subjects and passive beneficiaries, broadens the social gaps and heightens skepticism. It should not be surprising, therefore, that some authors argue that neither citizenship nor nationality are part of the identity of Mexico City's young residents (Ehernfeld Lenkiewicz 2003).

In our group, Mexican identity was closely linked to a sense of physical space with natural resources, history, and tradition, as well as to the way Mexican people relate with each other. Monica (F/15), from Machincuepa, defined her vision of being a Mexican:

I was born here, and I would give my life to defend [Mexico], because it is the place where I live side by side with all the people I love the most, and where I have my culture and my roots.

History as a key to gaining social consciousness was cited by Fernando (M/17), when he expressed his indignation at the reduction of history, civics, and geography classes in the high school curricula:

We are facing powerful interests of private enterprises and TV media to keep us in a bubble so that we may not learn about the really important matters. For example, one of the things that outrage me is the removal of history at school. What does this mean? We are not very literate, and now we are going backward. History is the only way to gain knowledge as to where we are at the present, where are we heading to, and what we can do. If they remove those contents, the government may want to fool us, maintaining us within the limits of our family sphere, or inside *antros* ("joints"). It's very convenient, so all of them won't let us have any political space, where decisions are taken.

Mexico has a political culture that naturalizes corruption as "short-cuts," as an expected and accepted way to resolve and "negotiate" the evasion of responsibilities (to bribe policemen when one commits a traffic infraction, to pay or offer a present to get faster attention in public offices, to give a few examples); many intellectuals have written about this political culture as part of the Mexican identity. Most of the participants in our study mentioned this as the roots of our problems and spoke of a generational opportunity to break this vicious circle.

This reality produced moral and ethical crises in many of the young people, who associated it with the double standards and hypocritical religious discourse previously mentioned:

There is a path defined by your values, but sometimes we don't see it to follow it. It is constructed throughout the years. . . . I wasn't conscious before and I questioned myself on the value of telling the truth, and what benefits would that bring me . . . getting there with the truth that would bring me problems instead of moving faster with a lie which nobody would notice and avoid the problems. . . . I learned that maybe one may go on but others may be harmed by your actions. (Alejandro M/16)

Politics is a farce . . . there is an urgent need to change the culture of corruption . . . from the president to us . . . we have been blinded . . . we classify people . . . and now we are talking about discrimination . . . we don't talk about gays, lesbians, single mothers, discrimination of poor people, of disabled people. . . . It took me by surprise to learn that one of the political candidates in Quebec was gay. (Basilio M/18)

Religions take advantage of the needs of the people and make money out of it. This is unjust. They preach "the word," about peace, and talk about moral issues when they . . . how should I put it? have double standards. . . . Religion is more a business than a faith issue, even though this may hurt and disappoint too many people. (Antonio M/23)

The young people we interviewed firmly rejected this way of making politics, because of the perceived incompetence and lack of credibility in the political discourses of actors and parties that seem very far from people and the social realities, which have resulted in apathy and mistrust in institutions. This opinion is shared by the youth and the general population, based on the high levels of exclusion and corruption in Mexican society (BID 2007; Flores 2003; Norris 2002; Ramos Lara 2006). Improvisation and incompetence are merely two of the defects that degrade politics; that is why Genaro (M/19), a student of political science in a private university, supported the regulation and formalization of a public administration career:

Once the citizen plays his role and the government official plays his, each will understand how they have to behave. A politician who was a boxer. How can he be a lawmaker? You have a certain kind of life; you cannot simply make the leap and become a congressman. We need to demand real professional politicians.

When asked about her position with regard to elections, Camila (F/16) said that misinformation made electoral participation meaningless:

I don't know well enough the political platform of the candidates . . . they attack each other and make clear that you must not vote for their oppositors, but they don't tell me why should I have to vote for them. They'd have to make clear somewhat the content of their political platform. I don't know what they're offering me, but I do know who they are casting aside; it doesn't make much sense and it's pretty hard [to know what they're talking about].

The lack of proposals and of a national project that goes beyond party interests affects how people vote, and then they vote for "the least worst," said Veronica (F/18), a member of Greenpeace.

Some of the young people said the growing political polarization prevented these topics from being addressed freely at home or among friends.

However, due to their engagement in social issues, many of them had managed to feel empowered and to develop a vision of legitimate, effective representation and political participation (Ávalos Tenorio 2006). Thus, Nora (F/13), the youngest participant, said that if any political action was to have an impact, it was necessary to mobilize and gather wide support. When we discussed the demand for a vote recount after the last presidential election, she talked about how the lack of a social consensus with respect to the official position prevented people from moving beyond party lines:

> If everyone reached an agreement, and only the government was wrong in refusing a recount, it would be right for people to go out and demonstrate. But it would have to be the whole country, something bigger. Right now, only two parties are discussing. It's a difficult problem.

Basilio (M/18) said he did not see himself as patriotic, but he said that the opportunity for change did not lie in changing the power structures but must spring from a grassroots movement: "If change in Mexico does not come from the people, from who we truly are, there will be no change, not ever. The problem is in us." And Carlos (M/17) reaffirmed this way of thinking: "There is no sense in blaming others for the problems that our country faces. We must assume our responsibility, or at least those who are implicated with their actions."

Antonio (M/23), a college student in sociology and an experienced activist, said the *partidocracia* (a term used to refer to the squabbling parties in Congress, which look after only their own interests), is one of the obstacles the system has designed to keep out citizens:

> This reform has to be done with the people, with citizens, with all social actors. Parties have their voice, but we as the people do not. I'd like a more participative, less representative kind of republic. If a person has, and I've seen this through the organization, good proposals, good ideas, and wants to do good for his country, the fact is, he's limited because he does not belong to a political party. Simply because he wants to uphold the right to have a different opinion, he is discriminated against. Simply because he wants to exercise that right. In Mexico, if you're not a member of a political party, there is nothing you can do for your country.

Alejandro (M/16) offered:

> We are in a society and politics are a means to act. . . . It's not only a matter of the government, although it certainly has to do with the government

because it has an influence on our society. But it's not only the government. I understand now there must be politics in a company, in an organization, politics at school, at home.

"We cannot remain indifferent," Lilia (F/15) said. "Decisions affect us all." And Juan (M/24) explained that he was searching for a political process of a universal and multidimensional nature, while Susana (F/20) summarized social conscience as follows: "What affects the other side of the world also affects you, because there's another human being out there, and because it's your world! The only planet you've got. You've got to consider that."

Young people situated themselves in this multidimensional time. Miriam (F/16) said:

I like history, I think, because I am Indian and all of Mexico's history began with the indigenous peoples. I read a lot, and I like to write. I like doing new things. Although sometimes, each time you fall, you think you're not going to get up again. But that was not the case. That taught me we have to continue to fight.

Graciela (F/18) envisioned herself acting in the public sphere based on her current awareness; the present is part of her future:

There are many things happening now, and the thought comes that tomorrow I'm going to have the chance to negotiate with many people, and I'll be able to change things that, right now, I don't believe are being done well or can be improved.

Although one-third of the participants in our project said they planned to migrate at some point in the future, in others a sense of nationalism that went beyond a sentimental or nostalgic attitude was deeply ingrained in their concept of social responsibility. As Julia (F/17) commented: "I plan to stay here. There are many things that need to be done here and I would be better able to reach my objectives here than in another country."

This viewpoint was shared by Miriam (F/16), the young indigenous migrant, even though she had several brothers living in the United States: "Despite everything, I like Mexico. Many might say, 'Then you like to suffer?' But that's not it. We should try to be better and make our country a better one. If we don't do it, nobody will."

The young people felt they could be part of a process that leads to transformation, and that time was on their side. "Adults may be doing what they can," said Susana (F/20), "but they have less time than we do to make things truly work."

Merleau-Ponty (1975 [1945]) conceives time as a network of intentionalities in which the idea is not only to share the present but also to keep in mind those "before me and after me" who will find themselves with similar questions or in the same "place of duration" that evokes the memory. Valencia García (2007) points out that multidimensionality is a condition inherent to this social period. Young people situate themselves in a world in which the past is integrated into the present. Machado Pais has explained it this way: "The past [historical time] is not only 'past' because it is no longer present, but rather because it refers to a specific series of events that a person has experienced and is 'carrying' in his/her present" (2000).

As Paulo Freire (2001) affirms, the importance of the social-historical assumption each person makes "to live history as a time of possibility" is what enables us to situate ourselves in a future that does not have to be the perpetuation of the present—of this present that causes so much indignation due to its injustice—and to envision utopia as a reality that is possible. As Juan (M/24) declared:

> I do not have a very clear idea of a future. But I like being in the present. In what I do now, in what I am doing. I feel the future will be built somehow. According to what you are doing right now in your present, you are building your future.

Notes

This study was carried out under a subcontract of the Metropolitan Autonomous University and the University of Illinois at Chicago thanks to the W. K. Kellogg Foundation's sponsorship; number P0118981; its contents are the sole responsibility of the author and do not necessarily represent the viewpoints of the W. K. Kellogg Foundation. I want to thank the Chapin Hall Center for Children at the University of Chicago for its support. I also want to thank Nathalie Coutu for her participation and assistance throughout all the phases of this research project.

1. That is the official age range that defines youth in Mexico in terms of social policies and demography.

2. A recent report made to the Committee of the Rights of Children states that there are around 780 foci of ungovernability localized in Mexico (Redim-Geremía 2011, 36).

3. Flores (2003) reports that according to the results of a national survey carried out by the Legal Research Institute of Universidad Nacional Autónoma de México (UNAM) in 2003, 56.7 percent of Mexican youth have no faith in public institutions, a basic component of democratic societies. Other studies confirm

this political skepticism on traditional and formal structures not only among youth but in the adult population as well. (Ramos Lara, 2007; Cuna Pérez, 2005, 2006; Tejera Gaona, 2006).

4. According to Cuna Pérez, "Between 1960 and 2000 four downtown districts registered a decrease of 43% of their youth population while the suburban districts increased it 300%" (2005, 80).

5. *Fresa* is a Mexican term, used also in Central America, to refer to a stereotype of youth focused on consumption, appearance, and status quo.

6. This proportion fits with recent city's statistical data: "In 1960, from every 100 households, 16 were headed by a woman; by 2000 it was 26 and by 2005, rose to 28.9 for every 100 households" (DF 2008, 565).

7. This perception about job prospects for those who finish school is in fact sustained by studies of youth and employment: while 42 percent of youth with a high school or subprofessional diploma are unemployed, only 29 percent of youth with a lower level of education are without a job. (Cordera Campos and Popoca García 2011; De Ibarrola 2009).

8. This perception aligns with Muñoz's study (1996, 83) of the Mexican population. He finds found that their aspirations are greater than expectations in groups with less schooling; people in groups with higher education have greater expectations and have certainty about the realization of their aspirations.

9. The Saintly Death is adored and worshiped especially by people whose lives are daily put at risk, such as drug traffickers, murderers, or other criminals; urban dwellers today also invoke this figure to protect and recover their health, stolen articles, and even family members who have been kidnapped. A well-known expert, Raúl Villamil, reflects on the symbolical displacement of devotion to this marginalized image, in which elements of Afro-Cuban Santeria can be found, as well as traces of a very popular colonial myth known as La Llorona (Weeping Woman), which was used at that time to inspire fear as a form of control (Cerón Montes de Oca 2007). The darkettos are followers of the dark movement, which unifies groups of people who identify with a philosophy of disenchantment, pessimism, and internal death. They dress in black and wear black makeup. The movement is derived from the British punk movement of the 1970s, and the followers are called *darks*, *gothics*, *vampires* (see Castillo Almaraz 2004).

10. The term *teacher* is in English in the original Spanish transcription. The insertion of English words is part of the young elite high-class speech code.

11. Wincour (2009) and García Canclini (2008) argue that these flexible and mobile strategies of social inclusion represent part of the symbolic capital that young people are acquiring: "They move fast in multiple directions and jump from one world to another, open several windows simultaneously and develop social and cognitive abilities to work, socialize and play in net, optimizing the links and shortcuts between one world and another" (Wincour 2009, 50).

References

Ávalos Tenorio, Gerardo. 2006. *El monarca, el ciudadano y el excluido: Hacia una crítica de lo político*. Mexico: UAM-Xochimilco.

Bartko, Todd. 2005. "The ABC of Engagement in out of School Time Programs." In "Participation in Youth Programs, Enrollment, Attendance, and Engagement." Special issue, *New Directions for Youth Development* 2005, no. 105 (Spring): 109–20.

BID (Banco Interamericano de Desarrollo). 2007. *Informe 2008: ¿Los de afuera? Patrones cambiantes de exclusión en América Latina y el Caribe: Informe Progreso Económico y Social 2008.* Edited by Gustavo Márquez. Washington, DC: BID and David Rockefeller Center for Latin American Studies.

Bolaños Sánchez, Ángel. 2006. "México/Niños indígenas sufren discriminación en escuelas." *Actualidad Étnica*, May 20. Retrieved from http://www.pagina digital.com.ar/articulos/2006/2006prim/educacion3/discriminacion-indigenas -educacion-200506.asp.

Butler, Udi, Marcelo Princeswal, and Roberta Abreu. 2007. *Culturas de Participacao: Jovens e suas Percepcoes e práticas de cidadania.* Rio de Janeiro: CIESPI (Centro Internacional de Estudos e Pesquisas Sobre a Infância).

Castillo Almaraz, Rosario. 2004. "Muerte y Futuro: El movimiento oscuro en el Tianguis Cultural del Chopo." *JOVENes Revista de Estudios sobre Juventud*, August 21, 86–109.

Castillo Berthier, Héctor . 1996. "Los proyectos juveniles: Entre la utopía y la cooptación política." *Las políticas sociales en México en los años noventa*, 365–93. Mexico: FLACSO (Facultad Latinoamericana de Ciencias Sociales), UNAM (Universidad Nacional Autónoma de México), and Instituto Mora-Plaza Valdés.

Cerón Montes De Oca, Javier. 2007. "La muerte: Un asunto de fiesta y devoción para los vivos." *Gaceta: Órgano informativo del Colegio de Bachilleres*, no. 8: 12–14. Retrieved from http://www.cbachilleres.edu.mx/cb/gaceta/pdf/g8.pdf.

Chaskin, Robert, and Stephen Baker. 2006. "Negotiating among Opportunity and Constraint: The Participation of Young People in Out-of-School Time Activities." Chicago: Chapin Hall Center for Children at the University of Chicago.

Clary, E. Gil, and Mark Snyder. 1999. "The Motivations to Volunteer: Theoretical and Practical Considerations." *Current Directions in Psychological Science* 8, no. 5: 156–59.

Cordera Campos, Rafael, and Alfredo Popoca García. 2011. "Desigualdad y juventud en México y América Latina". *Universidades*, UDUAL (Unión de Universidades de América Latina) 48: 72–82.

Cuna Pérez, Enrique. 2005. "Acerca de la desconfianza en las instituciones jóvenes y discriminación en la ciudad de México." *El Cotidiano* 20: 78–89.

———. 2006. "Reflexiones sobre el desencanto democrático: El caso de los partidos políticos y los jóvenes en la ciudad de México." *Sociológica* 21, no. 61: 95–134.

De Ibarrola, María. 2005. "Educación y trabajo." *Revista Mexicana de Investigación Educativa* 10: 303–13.

———. 2009. "El incremento de la escolaridad de la PEA en México y los efectos sobre su situación laboral y sus ingresos, 1992–2004." *Revista Electrónica de Investigación Educativa* 11, no. 2. http://redie.uabc.mx/vol11no2/contenido -deibarrola.html.

Del Río Lugo, Norma, and Nathalie Coutu, eds. 2007. *Jóvenes comprometidos en América.* Mexico: UAM-Xochimilco.

DF, Comité Coordinador para la Elaboración del Diagnóstico y Programa de Derechos Humanos del Distrito Federal. 2008. *Diagnóstico de derechos humanos del Distrito Federal*. Mexico: Comisión de Derechos Humanos del Distrito Federal.

Domínguez Pérez, Moisés, and Héctor Morales Gil De La Torre. 2003. "Políticas locales de juventud en México." In *Políticas públicas de Juventud en América Latina: Políticas locales*, edited by Óscar Dávila León. Valparaíso: Cidpa Centro de Estudios Sociales.

Durand Ponte, Víctor Manuel. 2004. *Ciudadanía y cultura política, México 1993–2001*. Mexico: Siglo XXI.

Ehernfeld Lenkiewicz, Noemí. 2003. "Los jóvenes y las familias: Encuentros y tensiones entre filiaciones e identidades." In Pérez Islas, 75–85.

Flanagan, Constance. 2003. "Developmental Roots of Political Engagement." *Political Science and Politics* 36, no. 2: 257–61.

Flores, Julia. 2003. "De apuestas, ganancias y pérdidas: Valores y creencias juveniles." In Pérez Islas, 147–85.

Freire, Paulo. 2001. *Pedagogía de la indignación*. Madrid: Morata.

García Canclini, Néstor. 2008. "Los jóvenes no se ven como el futuro: ¿Serán el presente?" *Revista Pensamiento Iberoamericano* 3, no. 2.

García Rojas, Fidel. 2007. "De joven a joven." In Del Río Lugo and Coutu 2007, 70–71.

Halpern, Robert, Gary Baker, and William Mollard. 2000. "Youth Programs as Alternative Spaces to Be: A Study of Neighborhood Youth Programs in Chicago's West Town." *Youth and Society* 31, no. 4: 469–506.

IMJ (Instituto Mexicano de la Juventud). 2006. *Encuesta Nacional de Juventud 2005: Resultados preliminares*. 23 Mexico: IMJ.

INEGI (Instituto Nacional de Estadística y Geografía). 2005. *II Conteo de Población y Vivienda*. Mexico: INEGI.

Knaul, Felicia Marie. 2002. "El impacto del trabajo infantil y la deserción escolar en el capital humano: Diferencias de género en México." In *La economía de género en México: Trabajo, familia, Estado y mercado*, edited by E. G. Katz and M. C. Correia. Mexico: NAFINSA-INMUJER (Nacional Financiera and El Instituto Nacional de las Mujeres).

Lomnitz, Larissa. 1975. Cómo sobreviven los marginados. Mexico: Siglo XXI.

Machado Pais, José. 2000. "Las transiciones y culturas de la juventud: formas y escenificaciones." *Revista Internacional de Ciencias Sociales*. 89–101.

Mendoza Ascencio, Marlen. 2007. "Nemilis ihuan to Tata: La vida es sólo una prueba de Dios." In Del Río Lugo and Coutu 2007, 45–54.

Merleau-Ponty, Maurice. 1975 [1945]. *Fenomenología de la Percepción*. Barcelona: Península.

Morales Razo, Noé. 2007. "Mi vida, aprendiendo el circo." In *Jóvenes comprometidos en América*, edited by Norma Del Río Lugo and Nathalie Coutu, 16–18. Mexico: UAM-Xochimilco.

Muñoz, H. 1996. *Los valores educativos y el empleo en México*. Mexico: CRIM-IIS (Instituto de Investigaciónes Sociales)-IDRC-UNAM (Universidad Nacional Autónoma de México) / Grupo Editorial Miguel Angel Porrúa.

Norris, Pippa. 2002. "La participación ciudadana: México desde una perspectiva comparativa." Retrieved from http://www.hks.harvard.edu/fs/pnorris/Acrobat/Mexican%20Civic%20Engagement%20Norris%20espanol.pdf Last access date, July 31, 2011.

OECD (Organisation for Economic Co-operation and Development). 2011. "Society at a Glance 2011: OECD Social Indicators." Retrieved from http://www.oecd.org/document/24/0,3746,en_2649_37419_2671576_1_1_1_37419,00.html.

Pérez Islas, José Antonio, ed. 2003. *México-Quebec: Nuevas miradas sobre los jóvenes.* Mexico: Instituto Mexicano de la Juventud and Centro de Investigación y Estudios sobre Juventud.

Pittman, Karen, Shanetta Martin, and Anderson Williams. 2007. *Core Principles for Engaging Young People in Community Change.* Washington, DC: Forum for Youth Investment, Impact Strategies.

Ramos Lara, Eleazar. 2006. "El estudio de la cultura política en México." In *Pensando la política: Representación social y cultura política en jóvenes mexicanos,* edited by Marco Antonio González Pérez, 91–118. Mexico: Plaza y Valdés.

———. 2007. "El imaginario político de los jóvenes en México: Notas para su reflexión." In *Política, etnicidad e inclusión digital en los albores del milenio,* edited by Scott Robinson Studebaker, Héctor Tejera Gaona, and Laura Valladares de la Cruz. México: UAM-Iztapalapa-Miguel Ángel Porrúa.

Redim-Geremía, V. 2011. *Infancia y conflicto armado en México: Informe alternativo sobre el protocolo facultativo de la Convención sobre los Derechos del Niño Relativo a la participación de niños en los conflictos armados.* Mexico: Red por los derechos de la Infancia en México; Infancia Cuenta; and Fundación para la Protección de la Niñez IAP.

San Juan, Carlos. 2006. "Democracias vacías: La apropiación por las elites del llamado gobierno del pueblo." In *Democracia y exclusión: Caminos encontrados en la Ciudad de México,* edited by Lucía Álvarez Enriquez, 31–42. Mexico: UNAM-UAM-A-UACM-INAH-Plaza y Valdés.

Serrano Pineda, Jorge. 2007. "Mi experiencia en el circo." In *Jóvenes comprometidos en América,* edited by Norma Del Río Lugo and Nathalie Coutu, 19–20. Mexico: UAM-Xochimilco.

STPS (Secretaría del Trabajo y Previsión Social) and INEGI (Instituto Nacional de Estadística y Geografía). 2010. "Módulo de trabajo infantil 2009." *Encuesta Nacional de Ocupación y Empleo 2009.* Documento metodológico. Mexico: STPS-INEGI.

Tejera Gaona, Hector. 2006. "Cultura ciudadana, gobiernos locales y partidos políticos en México." *Sociológica* 21, no. 61: 41–70.

Ulloa Herrero, Manuel I., and Manuel Ulloa Pizarro. 2006. *Las exclusiones de la educación básica y media superior en el D.F.* Mexico: Centro de Estudios en Economía de la Educación and UNICEF.

Valencia García, Guadalupe. 2007. *Entre cronos y kairós: Las formas del tiempo sociohistórico.* Mexico: Anthropos, UNAM.

Wincour, Rosalía. 2009. *Robinson Crusoe ya tiene celular.* Mexico: UAM-I-Siglo XXI eds.

World Bank. 2011. "Gross Domestic Product 2010." July 1. Retrieved from http://siteresources.worldbank.org/DATASTATISTICS/Resources/GDP.pdf.

FIVE

Emerging Political Identities, Practices, and Temporalities

Maria de los Angeles Torres, Irene Rizzini, and Norma Del Río

We set out to understand the trajectories, practices, and ideas of civically engaged youth in three cities of the Americas. The information we gathered in Rio de Janeiro, Chicago, and Mexico City showed a deep investment on the part of the young people. Their engagement may be positing new ideas about the place of young people in their political communities as well as redefining ways of being politically active. In this final chapter, we compare and contrast the ways in which the young people in our three cities became involved, what issues were important to them, how they acted upon those issues, and, finally, how they envisioned themselves in their political communities. While we cannot generalize beyond the particular interviews we conducted, we give ourselves the opportunity to reflect on what their trajectories and insights might add to our understanding of politically engaged young people, as well as what their activities may tell us about democratic practices in global cities in the Americas.

On Becoming Engaged

Early Influences

The young people's paths to civic engagement were many. Some were invited to a meeting by peers, others by relatives, many by community organizers, and still others by teachers. Nevertheless, most had at least a parent, or a significant adult, who listened to them and gave them permission to think independently. As a result, they felt valued early on in life. Families, however, could be ambivalent spaces. Some were encouraging, some discouraging, and some indifferent. It was not so much that many of the parents of the young people supported their activism, but rather that they gave their children permission to speak up and develop their own opinions. Indeed, some of the participants' parents in Mexico felt that activism would take time away from their children's studies or put the young girls at risk if they were traveling outside their neighborhood. In the United States, some parents were concerned that the children's engagement could draw attention to their families and might result in deportation. These young people had a special role in helping their families to navigate U.S. society; they had acquired a certain degree of authority about U.S. life that the adults ultimately needed and valued.

Being valued early on by their parents or a significant adult contributed to creating a strong sense of self and, perhaps most importantly, a feeling that their ideas were worthwhile. Their activism was supported by their strong sense of personal efficacy. Interestingly, in some families in Mexico, as the young people became involved in public organizations, their mothers joined their political causes. Other researchers had found similar patterns where mothers' political inclinations became more like their children's, in a way reversing predictions; the path of socialization in reality is complex and often contradictory (Langton 1966; Erikson 1994).

The reported influence of an adult in a young person's political development suggests the need to bring back into the study of political socialization the relevance of early childhood experiences, as other scholars have indicated (Sapiro 2004). Earlier approaches to socialization sought to find ties between early childhood development and political attitudes and ideas in later life (Flanagan and Sherrod 1998). In addition to focusing on the development of specific political attitudes and ideas as earlier studies did, it may be fruitful to explore the links between what makes children feel worthy within the family (or early in life) and what makes them decide to exercise this sense of worth in the public sphere. If activism is partly traced to the ways in which children are validated in the home, then efforts to increase the engagement of young people need to focus on parents and other adults and how they relate to children.

Institutions outside the Family

Schools and community organizations seem to play similar roles to those noted by other scholars (Andolina et al. 2003). Schools can be places where young people learn and where they pick up skills, particularly on debate teams and in classes, although most of the young people in our study were also involved in other school groups that allowed them to develop leadership and organizational skills. But our research shows that schools are far from the John Dewey model, in which adolescents experiment in organizing and deliberating important issues.

In Mexico, where studies have demonstrated a lack of relationship between levels of schooling and democratic culture (Fernandez Alatorre 2010), schools played a marginal role as promoters and educators of civic issues. Civic education was not based on debate practices or on building skills for participation. Instead, it was circumscribed to political rhetoric, which turns into meaningless texts when contrasted with the social and political reality of Mexico. The few democratic school practices organized by the Federal Electorate Institute have not been incorporated into the general curriculum (Ramírez 2005). Furthermore, student organizations in Mexico were not places of empowerment for young people. They were usually beholden to one political party or another and were perceived as tools of these parties.

The development of student movements in Brazil has a rich history that gives young people today a context (Mische 1997; Sousa 1999; Araújo 2007; Silva 2007; Caldeira 2008). The movements themselves provide spaces for engagement. Schools, however, were contested zones for many. The participants often defined them as a place where they lost their voice and one that did not prepare them for the future. Indeed, schools often forced rigid notions of citizenship (Tereshchenko 2007). Several of the young people interviewed in Rio de Janeiro were activists in school-related settings as part of the Movimento Estudantil Brasileiro (the Brazilian Student Movement) at the local, state, and federal levels. Their views were divided: schools could both enable their activism and create obstacles to it. Some mentioned their conflicts with professors and principals and how they were seen as troublemakers. A few were expelled from school because of their activism.

In Chicago, increased incidents of gang violence have turned schools into war zones, and administrators reacted by setting up hypervigilant practices and implementing invasive search and seizure procedures. This same climate of school violence prevails in many of the public schools of Mexico (Arrieta Archilla, Calderón Miyamoto, and Sauri Suárez 2007) and blocks the development of democratic practices, promoting in their place authoritarian ways of decision making (Monsiváis Carrillo 2002).

In contrast, community organizations in all three cities were safe zones that gave young people an opportunity to meet other committed peers. The organizations also gave them opportunities to learn political skills (Ginwright and Cammarota 2007) and to build social capital. Through community-based activities, they began to feel empowered as informed citizens. In Mexico, this was particularly true for women, who felt they could articulate their voices as they could nowhere else. Community organizations also provided stimulating political environments in which budding activism could find a collective expression. As they met young people from other areas, these youths were encouraged to be more open and forthcoming in accepting others who were different from them. Other researchers have found that these organizations become safe zones where young people feel they can be themselves (Halpern, Barker, and Mollard 2000). In Mexico, however, it seemed that it was more difficult to start a youth organization than in the other cities.

The organizations in which the participants in all three cities engaged were small. This was an important feature. In the midst of these huge urban areas, small, community-based organizations provided special anchors and gave young people a sense of belonging. Even though many of the young people were religious, we found that the young people we interviewed in Mexico and Chicago did not gravitate to religious organizations for their youth empowerment work. Rio was the exception. Perhaps the most striking example was that of a fifteen-year-old participant who was an active member of an important political party in Brazil. She was a member of the student movement in her school and was also active in her church, where she was responsible for teaching and organizing several activities. Religion has been identified as important for youth activism in Brazilian national surveys (Novaes and Campello Mello 2002; IBASE and Instituto Pólis, 2005) and can be an important element to the construction of their identities.

Self, Social, and Political Awareness

We were struck by the similarities in how the participants in all three cities described their awareness of their special characteristics as individuals. For most of them, the awareness that they might be different from others came early in life. Other scholars have also found that "Millennials" are confident, networked, and open to change (Taylor and Keeter 2010). Our participants could also be described that way, as they mentioned that, despite obstacles, they felt they could make a difference. They also referred to a strong a sense of curiosity, restlessness, and responsibility toward themselves, their families, and their communities.

In Rio de Janeiro, many of the participants had a sense of responsibility toward others, but not a paternalistic one. They had a strong sense of engaging in communal and cooperative activity for the good of the whole and rejected the idea of acting just for one's own benefit. There are key strands of collective and cooperative action in recent Brazilian history that could produce a stronger sense of the importance of such action in Brazilian youth than we found elsewhere. In contrast, in Chicago the responsibility was anchored in personal and familial spaces and, by extension, in the communities. In Mexico, young people also had a sense of commitment to their families and their neighborhoods.

Another common characteristic was our respondents' strong awareness of their age and how this tied them to other young people, although they stressed the fact that *young people* is not a term that describes a homogeneous group. Indeed, there were pluralities of experiences that defied one social category. Researchers have also cautioned about using *youth* as an all-encompassing category, and the participants in our study underscored this (Farthing 2010). Still, they were also aware that they were often excluded from political institutions because of their age, since many adults assumed that they were neither interested nor capable. But precisely because of that, they were also aware that if they defied the stereotypes, people would listen to them. Other people expected them not be articulate or intelligent about civic issues. The fact that they were made adults listen.

Social Identities

Politics is often played out as a group process, and groups often are defined by social characteristics. Historically, many of those characteristics have been used to exclude certain groups from political communities. For the young people we interviewed, age was this kind of characteristic. Some felt they were being discriminated against for other reasons, although those reasons differed from city to city. Class and race played an important part for some of the Brazilians. In Mexico City, young people had a strong sense of being *Mexicano*, even as they were keenly aware of the social identities that were lodged in distinct geographic communities. But it was in the United States that the sense of a political self was strongly connected with social identities. For nearly the first century of the country's history, only white male property owners were considered part of the political community. Struggles to expand that definition have succeeded in bringing in African Americans and women and also resulted in lowering the voting age to eighteen. Many of the movements that sought to broaden notions and practices of citizenship were organized along the very same social categories that had been used to exclude the groups, giving rise to "identity politics." Latino and African American youths expressed this sense of identity as they spoke of the need to represent their communities and to be included. Their sense of responsibility to represent their groups was closely tied to the perception that young people in general, and African Americans and Latinos in particular,

are portrayed negatively. Popular images of young people often characterized them as uncaring and apolitical, and if they were African American
or Latino, as violent as well. In part, their activism included creating an
alternate representation through practice and example. Some of the young
women felt that they did not have to represent all young women, but that
they did have to fight stereotypes in order to be heard. For Latinos, the
concept of ethnic and social identities had an important added dimension.
There has been debate among social scientists as to how and when Latinos
either choose national origin or pan-ethnic labels to identify themselves.
Some scholars have suggested that pan-ethnic labels are imposed from above
(Oboler 1985). Others, however, have suggested that the *Latino* identifier is
used as a cultural referent strategically, as an ethnopolitical category (Padilla
1985). Most of the young Latinos we interviewed chose a pan-ethnic label
that both brought them together with other young people of Latin American extraction and distinguished them from their homelands even as they
retained pride in their parents' homeland.

In Chicago, neighborhoods became important for the politics of young
people as well as for their sense of self. Neighborhoods in Chicago were
closely defined by the ethnic and racial composition of their residents. When
young people spoke of their communities, they were referring to their ethnic group as well. Many were keenly aware that their communities did
not receive the same treatment as others and that they were discriminated
against. What we did not find in Chicago was a close identification with
being *American*. For many, this national identity was problematic because
it represented being part of the success of the nation, something they felt
had eluded them.

In all three cities, there was a link between an awareness of discrimination and activism. Many talked about their feelings of indignation at social
injustices they or their friends and family had faced. Despite this awareness,
their membership in the different organizations turned out to be a positive
experience (Sanchez-Jankowski 2002; Pizarro 2005). In Mexico City, some
inverted a social stigma (physical appearance, type of language, physical
disability, indigenous origin, homosexuality) that had put them at risk of
discrimination and made it the motor of their social activism. Instead of
creating an obstacle to their activism, the social stigma became a source of
empowerment (Reguillo 2002; Ginwright 2005).

The activism of the young people contributed to building networks that
created resources for them and their communities (Akom 2006). Cultural
and gender-based identities were integral to their politics, and concerns
about racism and discrimination were central to their activism, but not

all-encompassing. Class, ethnic, racial, and social identities were not necessarily the defining dimension for the organizations in which they chose to participate, as they had been in the 1960s in the United States (Muñoz 1989).

Youth as a Political Category

For the young people in our study, age awareness helped transcend particular geographic, ethnic, and racial groups to create a community. That awareness of their "youth" has the potential to claim a political space in the present for young people who until now have been thought of as little adults-in-the-making. As a social category, it may have a unique place in postmodernity's temporality as well as in its borderless view of the world. It is also a social category that as Barnhurst (1998) has demonstrated through young people's narratives is constructed with multiple media points of reference that indeed are embedded with a series of Foucaultian instances of experiences and understandings about quotidian power relationships. Still as long as class, race, ethnicity, and gender create obstacles to equality, those social categories will intersect with age and become complex arenas where young people can struggle and indeed create political moments in the tradition of democratic politics.

These young activists had multiple points of reference (Burgess 2005). They were strategic about their social identities, which carried meaning and were embedded with historical weight. They deployed them strategically, depending on the circumstances. Some scholars have referred to these as hybrid identities (Nilan and Feixa 2006), but they can also be seen as a set of social tools embedded with narratives that allow the young people to move in and out of public discourses at the same time that they carve out their own political spaces.

Pivotal Political Moments

Broad political events in their respective countries were important in galvanizing many of the young people we interviewed, as these events piqued their interest in politics. In Chicago, for instance, the presidential elections of 2000, unique in that the Electoral College vote trumped the popular vote and created a political crisis, drew many young people's attention to politics. Another galvanizing event was Barack Obama's Senate race, which provided many young people with an opportunity to get involved in electoral politics for a candidate they believe was different. Obama's victory also encouraged them to continue their involvement, and many went on to work in his presidential campaign.

In its recent past, Brazil has experienced a number of events that led to new levels of political participation (Rizzini and Barker 2002). In 1989, the first direct election for the presidency of the republic was held after twenty-one years of military dictatorship. In 1993, the nation's political passions were aroused by the financial corruption of the president, Fernando Collor de Mello, who was impeached and removed from office. His removal followed massive street demonstrations against him by, among others, student activists. In 2002, the head of the most significant progressive party in Brazil, Luis Ignacio "Lula" da Silva of the Workers Party, was elected president after three unsuccessful attempts at that office.

In Mexico, the electoral defeat of the PRI (Partido Revolucionario Institucional) was defining a moment for many young people. Despite deep-seated distrust of political institutions and politicians, 71.8 percent of young citizens voted in the elections of July 2006 (Cordera Campos and Scheinbawn Lernier 2008). A recent study concluded that eighteen-year-olds saw themselves as capable of influencing the government in a greater proportion than Mexicans of older generations and that they felt capable of demanding accountability from the system (Moreno 2009).

The process of becoming engaged is not linear; it includes early and multiple influences as well as organizations on the ground available to youth. Context also matters, in that political moments can garner the attention of young people.

Civic Engagement: Issues, Practices, and Localities

Structural barriers that prevented young people in urban areas from having equal opportunities in life were of paramount concern for the young activists we interviewed (Bhimji 2005). They were keenly aware of what they needed in order to have an effective political voice and the obstacles that prevented them from attaining equality. In Chicago and in Rio, the most pressing issues they identified were related to education, including the deficiencies of the schools in the poorer communities and the students' lack of a voice in a place where so much of their lives unfold. In many ways, education is part of the democratic narrative regarding both the creation of a good citizen and the path to equality, and young people understand the linkage between educational attainment and political efficacy.

The young Mexicans in our study were aware that following an educational path rather than dropping out of school to try to find a job implied a long-term commitment and an uncertain future (Saraví 2009; Valenzuela

Arce 2009). They realized that education does not guarantee social mobility (UNDP 2010): more than a million young people enter the employment market each year in Mexico, (Meyer 1998), and those with higher education levels also have higher levels unemployment (Cordera Campos and Sheinbawn Lernier 2009; Cordera Campos and Popoca García 2011). Therefore employment opportunities were at the top of their agendas.

These young people were also intent on battling popular negative images, often involving racial and ethnic judgments, which they saw as obstacles to their being considered responsible citizens. (Rodriguez 2006; Trejo Sanchez et al. 2010). The young people saw a connection between how they were perceived and their lack of voice, and they set out to change those perceptions.

Practices

With a few exceptions, namely the young people involved in Mikva Challenge in Chicago and those with ties to political parties in Rio, the young activists we interviewed had not chosen the electoral arena as their primary political playing field. Many expressed similar opinions about electoral politics, including that politics had become a spectator sport in which the wealthy bid their way into office and influence. In Mexico, despite challenges by the PRI, the electoral system was still seen as corrupt and insulated from popular demands. The political parties were in crisis, crippled by an ideological blurring of principles and values and a focus on marketing to connect "with the maximum number of social sectors." However, even for those who were skeptical about the electoral arena, voting was considered a right and in some cases a responsibility, and many saw voting as a way to have their voices heard and also to keep politicians accountable. Furthermore, there were some indications that if a candidate who was perceived as genuinely committed appeared on the scene, young people would be inclined to participate in elections. Such was the case of Barack Obama in Chicago and Lula in Brazil. In Brazil, young activists did vote, as did most young people, even when the vote was not mandatory (Novaes and Campello Mello 2002).

We also looked at whether the political activism of young people was aimed at the state. In the United States, young people targeted government entities more than in Mexico. In Chicago, there was a sense of political entitlement and the perception of a right and a responsibility to hold government officials accountable that suggested the distance between citizen

17. Staging a protest play in Rio de Janeiro. Photo by Manuelle Rosa.

and state was not that far apart. The opposite was true in Mexico, where the distance between citizen and government is wide, and instead of feeling entitled to demand resources from the government, citizens rely on intermediaries to do so (Tejera Gaona 2006). This had the effect of creating what has been called low-intensity citizens, who felt entitled to show up only for the obligatory vote in national elections (O'Donnell 1999; Monsiváis Carillo 2002). In Rio, the focus of young people's advocacy depended to some degree on the organizations with which they were associated. But the government was a central target in some of the organizations, including the Landless Workers Movement, which had a large contingent of young members who regularly engaged with state and federal government officials.

The attitudes of the young people toward their governments and electoral politics led them to other arenas of activism, such as making films, participating in philanthropy, and organizing educational and community advocacy groups. In Mexico City in particular, young people seemed to use technology more readily and were involved in creating alternative media. Access to media and new social networking technologies turned out to be important tools to define their own social identities and perhaps even to create new virtual political communities (Feixa 2006). In all three cities, engaged young people understood the importance of working in the cultural arena. There was a sense that it was among cultural groups and in the media that ideas emanated. In addition, as cultural spaces and the media become important arenas for politics or what has been called the culturalization of politics (Reguillo 2005), the *public* has come to include these as well (Novaes and Vital 2006). That is why many scholars advocate that cultural activities need to be accessible to young people, so they can be seen as producers of culture rather than as objects of consumption (Castillo Berthier 2008).

Nongovernmental activities aimed at creating change contribute to the development of engaged citizens (Sherrod 2006). The young people in our study were involved in a variety of projects outside of electoral politics, and they had a strong sense of the impact they hoped to attain through their actions. As diverse as their forms of engagement were, they were more pragmatic than utopic. Some authors have suggested that this, too, is a product of postmodernity (Handler 1992). Indeed, by engaging in non-institutional settings and claiming the legitimacy of those spaces as political arenas, they were expanding the limits of what a good citizen could be (Gilbert 1992; Tamayo 2006).

The Style of Their Engagement

We were also struck by what could be called the young people's style of activism. In contrast to suggestions by many who study adolescent behavior that the political behavior of youth may be oppositional in nature, the young people we interviewed were thoughtful and respectful of others. Their desire to be respectful also included their desire to be informed. It was not so much that information influenced their activism, but rather that they believed that they should act from knowledge and not rashly. Tolerance of others and their beliefs was also a characteristic of almost all the youths interviewed. Their sense of rights and their style of politics were deeply embedded in a democratic tradition of debate and dissent. Furthermore, this respect for others gave them the ability to work with diverse people and enhanced their ability to form coalitions. They were politically agile in finding ways to have their voices heard and to create more equitable opportunities for themselves and others. We also noted that there were different degrees of engagement, and some of the young people made it clear that they did not always spend their time in these activities, but rather that they led balanced lives.

The Spaces of Their Engagement

There were commonalities, too, in terms of the spaces in which the young people's political engagement occurred in all three cities. Globalization promised to make the world a smaller place, and for activists that meant that their struggles could be thought of and acted out in a more unified fashion. For the youths in our three cities, their political understanding transcended national borders. In particular for the young people in Chicago, there was an awareness of the changing place of the United States in the world, as well as of the need to change the way the United States exercised its power—from one that readily used its military might to one more caring about the poor. The wars in Iraq and Afghanistan came up as one of their central concerns. In Mexico City and Rio, this global awareness was expressed in terms of the need for world peace and respect for human rights. Since 1965, when Brazil's military dictatorship supported the U.S. intervention in the Dominican Republic, the Brazilian army has been involved abroad only in humanitarian missions, so the issues of war and peace were not a concrete issue for activists in the country.

Globalization has also brought forth the increased mobility of labor and people. Immigration itself is a transnational, global issue that broadens people's perspectives beyond a particular nation-state. For young Latin Americans whose economic opportunities are limited, migration becomes a viable option. Migration from Mexico gave young people a postmodern vision in which time and spatial coordinates break down. For those who do migrate, the next step may be the reorganization of a transnational social identity that allows them to coexist and belong to two distinct worlds. This may also happen to the ones who do not migrate but have been touched by the massive migration of friends and relatives (Espinosa 1998; Del Rio Lugo 2007).

In the United States, growing numbers of young people are either immigrants themselves or the children of immigrants. They, too, inhabit transnational realities and do so with increasingly more awareness. But in the United States, even struggles around immigration are aimed at creating opportunities in the new country. The Dream Act, for which so many young Latinos campaigned, essentially combined the desire of young people for education with their need to become full members of their host country. For Mexico, emigration underscores the inability of the nation to provide opportunities and has become a rallying point to criticize the failure of the government to meet the promises of democracy.

Still, for most young people, politics unfolded in local settings—in schools and neighborhoods—even if they had global ties. The predominant identification was with community-based projects, not transnational ones. Their sights were set on institutions that affected their daily lives. Scholars who look at the scales of politics have suggested that it is in these specific localities that new forms of democracy are being formed. Globalization and the "global" may be too abstract a notion in which to forge new forms of politics (Esteva and Prakash 1998; Garcia Canclini 2004). This stands in contrast to other studies of young people in international solidarity movements that focus on countries other than theirs (Pollock 2006).

Class may play a role in the issues in which young people chose to participate. Unlike middle-and upper-class youth who may attend better schools and who are not generally objects of discrimination because of their socioeconomic status, working-class youth have to organize to receive even basic services in their schools, and this often becomes their primary focus. Class differences would be a worthy area of further study. Perhaps all activists are shaped by early influences, and their class positions lead them to different issues.

During the final stages of our study, the availability of social media grew markedly, and so did its use in political advocacy and organizing, particularly for young people. This can have an impact on both political practices and the spaces of engagement. It also raises many interesting questions about the role of social media in changing the nature of participation, bringing it more in line with ways in which young people interact (Young 2007). Does participation become more individual or more social? Are there new identities that emerge from engaging virtually? There are also questions about how to best use social media to increase participation (Burd 2010). Clearly, in political elections, get-out-the-vote campaigns aimed at young people have effectively used new social media to mobilize. We think these questions are critical to a fuller understanding of youth activism, even though we believe that the dynamics of how young people engage in civic action may follow similar paths regardless of what tools they use. It is an area for future research.

In a way, the young people we interviewed had internalized the language and promise of modernity in their political activities: They claimed the right to equal representation, regardless of race, gender, or ethnicity. Their concerns about their place in popular culture and about how they are socially constructed are closely tied to the current era of information and images. They have developed strategies that overlap traditional politics and newer forms of political activism that are more flexible and less corporatively hierarchal (Serna 1998; Novaes and Mello 2002). Yet their struggles for equality

18. Mikva students campaigning and reporting. Photo by Mikva Challenge.

and for fair cultural representations tie them to a community that is still very much defined by neighborhood geography (Skelton and Valentine 1998). Their concerns hearken back to the promises of modern democracies, but their struggles are waged with new forms of organizations and practices; indeed, with new social media this will probably be further accentuated.

Envisioning: Their Political Ideas

Questioning the Temporality of Modernity

One of the most striking similarities in our participants' views about politics was their sense of entitlement in the present. They were clearly aware that their societies situated them in the future, and that politicians talked about them as the future of their country, without giving them a voice in the present. Therefore, they extracted agency in the present. They wanted to be heard now, wanted to exercise their rights now, and wanted to be considered citizens, with rights, now. Some of this derived from a strong sense of the difficulties and dangers that young people in urban areas faced. They saw themselves as capable members of a political community with problems that needed to be resolved today, not tomorrow. They also felt that by being placed in the

19. Rio de Janeiro youth protest. Photo by Manuelle Rosa.

future, they were being ignored. While they appreciated their links to history and heritage, and their impending role in a future society, the present was the place from where they spoke, and it was where they wanted to have a say. This temporality stands in sharp contrast to the place modernity made for children and youth as future citizens, without rights in the present, and is, indeed, a critique of its political projects. The young people's urgency is, in effect, a contestation of the nation itself (Woo 2005; Garcia Canclini 2008), for nations have their own temporalities, and by placing citizens in the future, they basically retain power in the present (Shapiro 2000).

Rights

Rights are embedded in the notion of citizenship. Some of the young people in Mexico were aware of existing legislation regarding the rights of children and youth, and one had been involved in crafting language for a United Nations document on the rights of indigenous children and youth. There was a strongly pronounced sense of youth rights in Rio, as well. The conditions of people living in low-income communities, or *favelas*, were an immediate, everyday reminder of the hardships many people suffered at home. Accordingly, much of the work of the activists in Rio was directed at alleviating difficult and violent conditions in their own backyards. That work was couched in the language of rights, but the locus of that sense of rights was the Brazilian Constitution of 1988 and the 1990 Statute on the Child and Adolescent, both of which included various, specific sets of rights. For instance, the Statute on the Child and Adolescent's Article 53, concerning education, lists the following rights: equality of conditions for access and permanence in school; the right to be respected by their educators; the right to contest criteria of evaluation, together with the right to appeal to a higher educational jurisdiction; the right to organize and participate in student entities; access to a public school near the student's residence and free of charge. The key provisions of the United Nations Universal Declaration of Human Rights—which had been under discussion when Brazil wrote its own documents—are listed on separate, large billboards in a major downtown park in Rio. The notion of rights is thus a constant element of political and activist discourse in the country (Kaufman and Rizzini 2009).

For youth in the United States, freedom of speech and expression is a fundamental right granted by the First Amendment of the Constitution. While a few young people mentioned collective rights such as education and health care, the right to protest and act politically was on the top of their list. Democratic citizenship for them included the right, and indeed the responsibility, to dissent (Maira 2004). There was also an understanding that there are public and private spaces in a person's life, and as fluid as these may be, there are differences in the kinds of rights and limitations inherent in each.

The young people we interviewed in Chicago tended to identify their rights as individual rights, broadly conceived as civil liberties and civil rights—that is, rights that protect individual actions from government censorship or that empower citizens to participate in government. Voting, particularly for African American teenagers, was seen as a historical responsibility; it might not make a difference, but not voting was self-defeating. Latinos argued the vote was something everyone should have, regardless of legal status. The right to education was also identified by the young people in Chicago, who saw education as necessary in order to exercise civil liberties and civil rights.

The contrast among the three cities is telling. The young people we interviewed in Rio and Mexico placed a greater emphasis on economic and social rights, specifically youth and children's rights. In these countries, social rights have been part of the political rhetoric, as states have tried to bridge the gaps between rich and poor that historically were more profound in Latin America (Quiroga 2002; Tamayo 2006; Trejo Sanchez et al. 2010).

Inclusive Political Communities and Expectations about the Place of Government

In all three cities, young people used more traditional language to cite the need for political communities to be more inclusive of young people in general. In Chicago, this included young immigrants who by the nature of their legal status were not granted full rights. Those from immigrant communities felt strongly that everyone who contributed to society should be allowed to vote, regardless of legal status. Underlying these beliefs was a deep commitment to the principle of equality, which was almost universally shared by the young people in all three cities (Dagnino 2007; Reguillo 2005). This reflects a modernist impulse to be inclusive and to expand notions of who is entitled to belong to political communities.

The sum of the youths' political views could be discerned from their definitions of a good government. In Chicago, young people thought a good government was more inclusive, more helpful, more globally responsible. Most striking was their idea that government was not static and needed to take into account social changes.

In Brazil, long opposition to military rule still colored attitudes toward government, even democratic governments. The young people interviewed in Rio defined good government as transparent and responsible to all including the poor. In Mexico City, activists wanted a government that made decisions by consulting with citizens. In all three cities, of course, young people said it was desirable to have a government that took their generation into account.

Altruism or Pragmatism

Historically the activism of young people has been linked with idealism, altruism, and rebellion (Luzzatto 1997). The activists of the 1960s, a common point of reference for activists today, thought of political change in utopian ways. The young people we interviewed for this project seemed to be more realistic, pragmatic, and willing to work within their communities and political systems. They were flexible with their ideas. They did not posit their political project in grandiose terms. Rather they sought a more democratic political process, one that provided equal opportunities and included a place for them in public life. There were more specific proposals for inclusion in forms of government that purported to represent all people. In addition, the altruism that shrouded the grand transformative projects of the 1960s was not as predominant with these youths. Altruism was coupled with a sense of obligation to their own community. This is not to say that they were unconcerned about the well-being of others, but their concerns were rooted in the interests of their groups, injecting their projects with a sense of real politics (Subirats 2004).

The young activists in Rio did use more altruistic language. Most of them showed deep interest in helping others, and the word *help* appeared quite often in the interviews, though it has several meanings. For example, to be involved politically meant to help others; participation meant to insert one-self in the social environment and help the process of constructing society.

Overall, these young activists are not pursuing utopian projects like those that characterized the social movements in the 1960s (Keniston 1968). Even those young people in Rio who made references to fighting for a better world had visions of a world that fulfilled the promises of democracy; they were not necessarily aiming to create an ideal place (Soares 2010). The twenty-first century seems to have brought forth sobered young activists. Perhaps it was their working-class background that grounded them in a more real politics in comparison to youth of the 1960s. Or perhaps it was the failure of twentieth-century utopian projects that resulted in more realistic expec-tations on the part of the new generation. Whatever the reason, the young people's practices suggest alternative ways of thinking about some of the basic tenets of democracy.

Democratic Practices in Global Cities in the Americas: At the Crossroads

Democracy has many meanings, but essential to all of them is a deliberative process that is inclusive of its members. These young activists are reclaiming a place in these processes. They are also demanding equality for themselves and their communities.

A study similar to ours, done in Quebec, revealed that the young people in that Canadian province were pragmatic in their politics (Quéniart 2008); the issues were more important than the organizations in which they par-ticipated. They were also involved in trying to make their province more democratic by bringing citizens and elected officials closer and were search-ing for ethical consistency that could give meaning to the values they shared.

The young people we interviewed also shared these core values. Their activism was fueled by their awareness of structural inequalities and dis-crimination. This awareness helped them develop social identities and com-munities and became a bridge to political action. Their social identities were embedded in the history and culture of each country, but in all three cities the concept of youth as a political and social category had a power-ful meaning for the young people, even as they recognized that the term did not encompass a homogeneous group. For them, youth transcended national borders, and they found similarities with peers around the world. As they focused on local issues, they were aware of the global implications of the politics of the country in which they lived, and they sought a less militaristic government that was responsible toward the poor locally and globally (Esteva and Prakash 1998).

In some cases, they were involved in traditional political activities. Many, however, went outside traditional forms of participation, expanding the boundaries of the political as they sought to influence decisions that affected them and to change images that distorted who they were. In the process, they were developing new ways of practicing citizenship, even as the rights they assumed to be part of this were distinct in each country (Corona Caraveo and Linares Pontón 2007). Essentially, what defined their politics was an insistence on inclusion and fairness and a vision that included a place for the state in the lives of people, especially in providing for the neediest.

Their practices led to the formation of communities that sometimes were defined by their age, at other times by their geographic urban locations, and at still other moments by their racial and ethnic backgrounds—often these coexisted. Still they formed communities that allowed them to act collectively and have an effective voice (Hart 2009).

A unique feature of their ideas was that they should be dealt with in the present. They would not be "Future Citizens" (Niemi 1974). If their role was limited to their future potential, they insisted, they would be denied rights and guarantees in the present. Indeed, without protections in the present, they would be vulnerable, particularly in a moment where *youth* is socially constructed in negative ways.

In sum, these young people moved easily between modernist constructions of politics—equality, for example—while demanding a new temporality that was highly critical of modernity's placement of youth in the future (Shapiro 2000). But even this postmodernist impulse was grounded in modernist promises of inclusive political communities, with guarantees of equality. As such, we can say that they are at the crossroads of modernity's promises and postmodernist ways of being political.

There are many discussions under way about how to bring children and young people into the political process (Youniss and Levine 2009). Those committed to the idea of a democracy of informed and engaged individuals may need to consider both the home and certain institutions as places to nurture that engagement. The home may provide an environment where young people are instilled with a sense of the public self. At the same time, the institutions in which their lives evolve may provide ways for them to

20. At the end of a protest. Photo by Manuelle Rosa.

have a voice, thus encouraging a type of engagement that has meaning for them in the present.

In terms of policies, this means that a focus on youth empowerment that does not include the home and the family may be incomplete (O'Donoghue and Stroble 2007). Parents need to be brought into "youth empowerment" projects. Giving children the space at home to articulate their ideas and be heard helps them develop confidence and perhaps expectations that this is the way they should always be treated. Most of the projects we encountered in our research in Rio de Janeiro, Mexico City, and Chicago were aimed exclusively at youth and not at families.

On the other hand, schools have the potential of developing practices that give young people a say in what goes on in those institutions. (Quinn 2011). While John Dewey's vision is still relevant today, in reality very few schools have developed a culture of democracy or employ democratic methods. This is particularly true in public schools in working-class communities.

The message simply is that if a society wants civically engaged adults, children need to be nurtured and their ideas respected. And as Hannah Arendt suggested, engaged individuals build effective political communities that maximize the ability of each individual to attain freedom.

These narratives suggest that young people are finding ways to engage in public affairs that deeply affect their lives. They want to be included in decisions that touch them, especially in their communities and in their schools. They also do not want to be lumped into a rigid category that may distort who they are individually or collectively, since they believe that stereotypes hinder their ability to be taken seriously. These young people demonstrate a mature concern for an informed and a responsible activism, an attitude that seems to be born in their relationship with their parents or with significant adults early in life and then nurtured by community-based organizations. In the process, they are developing a political culture of tolerance for others and agency for themselves. They are practicing democrats, citizens in the present.

References

Akom , A. A. 2006. "The Racial Dimensions of Social Capital: Toward a New Understanding of Youth Empowerment and Community Organizing in America's Urban Core". In *Beyond Resistance! Youth Activism and Community Change: New Democratic Possibilities for Practice and Policy for America's Youth*, edited by Shawn Ginwright, Pedro Noguera, and Julio Cammarota, 81–92. New York: Routledge.
Andolina, Molly W., Krista Jenkins, Cliff Zukin, and Scott Keeter. 2003. "Habits from the Home, Lessons from School: Influences of Youth Civic Engagement." *PS: Political Science & Politics* 36, no. 2: 275–80.
Araújo, Maria Paula Nascimento. 2007. *Memórias estudantis, 1937–2007: Da fundação da UNE aos nossos dias*. Rio de Janeiro: Editora Relume Dumará / Fundação Roberto Marinho.
Arrieta Archilla, Ainara, Sayuri Calderón Miyamoto, and Gerardo Sauri Suárez. 2007. *Derechos de la infancia en el D.F.: Diagnóstico de los derechos de los niños y niñas en el D.F.: Agenda de política pública para la infancia en el D.F.* Mexico: Red por los Derechos de la Infancia en México, CDHDF (Comisión de Derechos Humanos del Distrito Federal), and Indesol (Instituto Nacional de Desarrollo Social).

Barnhurst, Kevin G. 1998. "Politics in the Fine Meshes: Young Citizens, Power and Media." *Media, Culture and Society* 20, no. 2: 201–18. Retrieived from http://mcs.sagepub.com/content/20/2/201.

Bhimji, Fazila. 2005. "Latino/a Youth Contest for Equity in the Public School System in Boyle Heights, Los Angeles: A Political and Theoretical Perspective." In *Contemporary Youth Research: Local Expressions and Global Connections*, edited by Helena Helve and Gunilla Holm. Hants, UK: Ashgate.

Burd, Leo. 2010. "Developing Technological Initiatives for Youth Participation and Local Community Engagement." *New Directions for Youth Development*, no. 128, 95–104.

Burgess, Thomas. 2005. "Introduction to Youth and Citizenship in East Africa." *Africa Today* 51, no. 3: 7–24.

Caldeira, Paula. 2008. "Narrativas de jovens engajados no movimento estudantil e em partidos políticos na cidade do Rio de Janeiro: Um olhar a partir da Teoria do Reconhecimento Social." Diss., UFRJ (Universidade Federal do Rio de Janeiro).

Castillo Berthier, Hector. 2008. *Juventud, cultura y política social: Un proyecto de investigación aplicada en la ciudad de México, 1987–2007*. México: IMJUVE-SEP.

Cordera Campos, Rafael, and Alfredo Popoca García. 2011. "Desigualdad y juventud en México y América Latina." *Universidades*, UDUAL (Unión de Universidades de América Latina y el Caribe), no.48: 72–82.

Cordero Campos, Rafael, and Diana Sheinbawn Lernier. 2008. "Juventud y participación ciudadana." *Este País,* no. 217 (April): 21–36.

Corona Caraveo, Yolanda, and María Eugenia Linares Pontón. 2007. "Promoting Children and Youth Participation in the Creation of Citizenship." *Children, Youth and Environments* 17, no. 2: 1–10. Retrieved from http://www.colorado.edu/journals/cye.

Dagnino, Evelina. 2007. "Dimensions of Citizenship in Contemporary Brazil." *Fordham Law Review* 75, no. 5: 2469–82. Retrieved from http://ir.lawnet.fordham.edu/flr/vol75/iss5/7.

Del Río Lugo, Norma. 2007. "La transformación posible: Del uso segregador de los espacios a formas negociadas de convivencia." In *Niñez y Juventud: Dislocaciones y mudanzas*, edited by Norma Del Río Lugo, 129–43. Mexico: UAM-Childwatch International Research Network.

Erikson, Erik H. 1994 [1968]. *Identity: Youth and Crisis*. New York: Norton.

Espinosa, Victor. 1998. *El dilema del retorno: Migración, género y pertenencia en un contexto transnacional*. Mexico: El Colegio de Michoacán—El Colegio de Jalisco.

Esteva, Gustavo, and Madhu Suri Prakash. 1998. *Grassroots Post-Modernism: Remaking the Soil of Cultures*. London: Zed Books.

Farthing, Rys. 2010. "The Politics of Youthful Antipolitics: Representing the 'Issue' of Youth Participation in Politics." *Journal of Youth Studies* 13, no. 2: 181–95.

Feixa, C. 2006. "Generación XX: Teorías sobre la juventud en la era contemporánea." *Revista Latinoamericana de Ciencias Sociales, Niñez y Juventud* 4, no. 2: 3–18.

Fernández Alatorre, A. C. 2010. *Formación ciudadana e identidad. Voces de la sociedad civil*. México: Universidad Pedagógica Nacional.

Flanagan, Constance, and Lonnie Sherrod. 1998. "Youth Political Development: An Introduction." *Journal of Social Issues* 54, no. 3 (Fall): 447–56.

García Canclini, N. 2004. *Diferentes, desiguales y desconectados: Mapas de la inter-culturalidad*. Barcelona: Gedisa.

———. 2008. "Los jóvenes no se ven como el futuro: ¿Serán el presente?" *Revista Pensamiento Iberoamericana*, no. 3.

Gilbert, R. 1992. "Citizenship, Education and Postmodernity." *British Journal of Sociology of Education* 13, no. 1: 51–68.

Ginwright, Shawn. 2005. "Toward a Politics of Relevance: Race, Resistance and African American Youth Activism." In *Youth Activism: A Web Forum Organized by the Social Science Research Council* . Retrieved from http://ya.ssrc.org/african/Ginwright/.

Ginwright, Shawn, and Julio Cammarota. 2007. "Youth Activism in the Urban Community: Learning Critical Civic Praxis within Community Organizations." *International Journal of Qualitative Studies in Education* 20, no. 6 (November–December): 693–710.

Halpern, Robert, Gary Barker, and William Mollard. 2000. "Youth Programs as Alternative Spaces to Be: A Study of Neighborhood Youth Programs in Chicago's West Town." *Youth and Society* 31, no. 4: 469–506.

Handler, Joel. 1992. "Postmodernism, Protest, and the New Social Movements." *Law and Society Review* 26, no.4: 697–732.

Hart , Stella. 2009. "The 'Problem' with Youth: Young People, Citizenship and the Community." *Citizenship Studies* 13, no. 6: 641–57.

IBASE (Instituto Brasiliero de Análises Sociais e Econômicas) and Instituto Pólis. 2005. *Juventude Brasileira e Democracia: Participação, esferas e políticas públicas*. Rio de Janeiro: IBASE.

Kaufman, Natalie Hevener, and Irene Rizzini. 2009. *Globalization and Children: Exploring Potentials for Enhancing Opportunities in the Lives of Children and Youth*. New York: Springer.

Keniston, Kenneth. 1968. *The Young Radicals: Notes on Committed Youth*. New York: Harcourt, Brace and World.

Langton, Kenneth P. 1966. "Political Partisanship and Political Socialization in Jamaica." *British Journal of Sociology* 17, no. 4: 419–29.

Luzzatto, Sergio. 1997. "Young Rebels and Revolutionaries, 1789–1917." In *A History of Young People in the West,* vol.2, edited by Giovanni Levi and Jean-Claude Schmitt. Translated by Camille Naish. Boston: Belknap Press of Harvard University.

Maira, Sunaina. 2004. "Youth Culture, Citizenship and Globalization: South Asian Muslim Youth in the United States after September 11. *Comparative Studies of South Asia, Africa and the Middle East* 24, no. 1: 229–31.

Meyer, Lorenzo. 1998. "Los jóvenes y el fin de siglo mexicano." In *México: Diálogo entre generaciones*, edited by Francisco Orvañanos, 15–21. México: Oceano.

Mische, Ann. 1997. "De estudantes a cidadãos: Redes de jovens e participação política." *Revista Brasileira de Educação*, no. 5/6: 134–50.

Monsiváis Carrillo, Carlos Alejandro. 2002. "Ciudadanía y juventud: Elementos para una articulación conceptual." *Perfiles Latinoamericanos*, no. 20, 157–76.

Moreno, Alejandro. 2009. "La generación polarizada." *Este País*, no. 217 (April), 48–51.

Munoz, Carlos. 1989. *Youth, Identity, Power: The Chicano Movement*. New York: Verso.

Niemi, Richard G ., ed. 1974. *The Politics of Future Citizens*. San Francisco: Jossey-Bass.

Nilan, Pam, and Carles Feixa, eds. 2006. *Global Youth? Hybrid Identities, Plural Worlds*. New York: Routledge.

Novaes, Regina, and Cecília Campello Mello. 2002. Jovens do Rio: Circuitos, crenças e acessos. Rio de Janeiro: Comunicações do ISER, no. 57.

Novaes, Regina, and Christina Vital. 2006. "Today's Youth: (Re)Inventions in Social Participation." In *Partnering with Youth to Build the Future*, edited by Andrés Thompson, 101–40. Sao Paolo: Peiropolis-Kellogg Foundation.

Oboler, Suzanne. 1985. *Ethnic Labels, Latino Lives: Identity and the Politics of (Re) Presentation in the United States*. Minneapolis: University of Minnesota Press.

O'Donnell, Guillermo.1999. "Horizontal Accountability in New Democracies." In *The Self-Restraining State: Power and Accountability in New Democracies*, edited by Andreas Schedler, Larry Diamond, and Marc F. Plattner, 29–52. Boulder, CO: Lynne Rienner.

O'Donoghue, Jennifer L. and Karen R. Strobel. 2007. "Directivity and Freedom: Adult Support of Activism among Urban Youth." *American Behavioral Scientist* 51, no. 3: 465–85.

Padilla, Felix. 1985. *Latino Ethnic Consciousness: The Case of Mexican Americans and Puerto Ricans in Chicago*. Notre Dame, IN: University of Notre Dame Press.

Pizarro, Marcos. 2005. *Chicanas and Chicanos in School: Racial Profiling, Identity Battles, and Empowerment*. Austin: University of Texas Press.

Pollock, Mica. 2006. "Struggling for Solidarity: The 'International Solidarity Movement' as a Snapshot of Transnational Youth Activism." *Youth Activism: A Web Forum Organized by the Social Science Research Council*. Retrieved from http://ya.ssrc.org/transnational/Pollock/.

Quéniart, Anne. 2008. "The Form and Meaning of Young People's Involvement in Community and Political Work." *Youth and Society* 40, no. 2: 203–23.

Quinn, Brandy. 2011. "The School as a Democratic Community." *Applied Development Science* 15, no. 2: 94–97.

Quiroga, Ana Maria. 2002. "A Cidadania como indicador social." In *Juventud, Cultura e Cidadania. Comunicacoes do ISER* 21, special issue.

Ramirez, Gloria. 2005. *La educación ciudadana ante los retos de la democracia en México*. Mexico: UNESCO.

Reguillo, Rossana. 2002. "Cuerpos juveniles, políticas de identidad." In *Movimientos juveniles en América Latina: Pachucos, malandros, punketas*, edited by Carles Feixa, Fidel Molina, and Carles Alsine. Barcelona: Ariel.

———. 2005. *Horizontes fragmentados, comunicación, cultura, pospolítica: El (des) orden global y sus figuras*. Tlaquepaque, Jalisco, Mexico: ITESO (Instituto Tecnológico y de Estudios Superiores de Occidente).

Rizzini, Irene, and Gary Barker. 2002. "Promises Kept, Promises Broken: Recent Political and Economic Trends Affecting Children and Youth in Brazil." In *Globalization and Children: Exploring Potentials for Enhancing Opportunities in the Lives of Children and Youth*, edited by Natalie H. Kaufman and Irene Rizzini, 129–50. New York: Kluwer Academic/Plenum.

Rodríguez, M. Á., ed. 2006. *Testimonios de discriminación: Historias vivas*. México: CGEIB (Coordinación General de Educación Intercultural y Bilingüe), SEP,

Contracorriente, UPN (Universidad Pedagógica Nacional), FLAPE (Foro Lati-noamericano de Políticas Educativas), and Observatorio ciudadano de la Educación.

Sanchez-Jankowski, M. 2002. "Minority Youth and Civic Engagement: The Impact of Group Relations." *Applied Developmental Science* 6, no. 4: 237–45.

Sapiro, Virginia. 2004. "Not Your Parents' Political Socialization: Introduction for a New Generation." *Annual Review Political Science* 7: 1–23.

Saraví, Gonzalo A. 2009. *Transiciones vulnerables: Juventud, desigualdad y exclusión en México*. México: CIESAS (Centro de Investigaciones y Estudios Superiores en Antropologia Social).

Serna, Leslie. 1998. "Globalización y participación juvenil: En búsqueda de el-ementos de reflexión." *JOVENes*, no. 5, 42–57.

Shapiro, M. J. 2000. "National Times and Other Times: Rethinking Citizenship." *Cultural Studies* 14, no. 1: 79–98.

Sherrod, Lonnie R. 2006. "Promoting Citizenship and Activism in Today's Youth." In *Beyond Resistance! Youth Activism and Community Change: New Democratic Possibilities for Practice and Policy for America's Youth*, edited by Pedro Noguera, Shawn Ginwright, and Julio Cammarota, 287–300. New York: Taylor & Francis.

Silva, Izabel Priscila Pimentel da. 2007. Jovens, estudantes e rebeldes: A construção das memórias estudantis. Caderno de Resumos. *Encontro Regional Sudeste de História Oral—Memória e Política* 7. Rio de Janeiro: Anais.

Skelton, Tracey, and Gill Valentine, eds. 1998. *Cool Places: Geographies of Youth Cultures*. London: Routledge.

Soares, Bárbara A. 2010. "Sentidos y prácticas de participación juvenil en contex-tos de exclusión: El caso brasileño." Paper presented at the Calidad de vida y derechos de niños, niñas y jóvenes en América Latina. VI Conferencia Inter-nacional—Red Childwatch Latinoamérica y el Caribe/III Jornada del Programa de Investigación en Calidad de Vida.

Sousa, Janice Tirelli Ponte de. 1999. *Reinvenções da utopia: A militância política de jovens nos anos 90*. São Paulo: HackerEditores / FAPESP.

Subirats, Joan. 2004. "La implicación social ante los retos de la exclusión." Re-trieved from http://unpan1.un.org/intradoc/groups/public/documents/CLAD/clad0044517.pdf.

Tamayo, Sergio. 2006. "Espacios de ciudadanía, espacios de conflicto." *Sociológica*, 21, no. 61: 11–40.

Taylor, Paul, and Scott Keeter, eds. 2010. *Millennials: Confident. Connected Open to Change*. Pew Research Center.

Tejera Gaona, Héctor. 2006. "Cultura ciudadana, gobiernos locales y partidos políticos en México." *Sociológica* 21, no. 61: 41–70.

Tereshchenko, A. 2007. "National and Regional Citizenship Identities: A Study of Post-Communist Youth." In *Citizenship Education in Society*, edited by A. Ross, 699–712. London: CiCe.

Trejo Sánchez, Jose Antonio, Jorge Arzate Salgado, and Alicia Itatí Palermo, eds. 2010. *Desigualdades sociales y ciudadanía desde las culturas juveniles en América Latina*. México: UAEM-Miguel Angel Porrúa.

UNDP (United Nations Development Programme). 2010. *Informe Regional sobre Desarrollo Humano para América Latina y el Caribe 2010: Actuar sobre el futuro:*

romper la transmisión intergeneracional de la desigualdad. San José, Costa Rica: UNDP.

Valenzuela Arce, J. M. 2009. *El futuro ya fue: Socioantropología de l@s jovenes en la modernidad*. Mexico: El Colegio de la Frontera Norte-Casa Juan Pablos.

Woo, Yen Yen Joyceln. 2005. "Remaking Citizens' Perspectives from the Lived Temporalities of Four Singapore Youths." In *Contemporary Youth Research: Local Expressions and Global Connections*, edited by Helena Helve and Gunilla Holm, 173–84. Hants, UK: Ashgate.

Young, Brian D. 2007. *Young Citizens in the Digital Age: Political Engagement, Young People and New Media*. Abingdon: Routledge.

Youniss, James, and Peter Levine. 2009. *Engaging Young People in Civic Life*. Nashville, TN: Vanderbilt University Press.

Appendix. Details on Study Participants

Chicago

Pseudonym	Gender	Age	Race/Ethnicity	Activities	Organizations
Maceo	M	13	Latino	Video Documentaries/Immigration	Video Machete
Lilian	F	13	Latino	Video Documentaries/Immigration	Video Machete
Dante	M	11	Latino	Video Documentaries/Immigration	Video Machete
Omar	M	17	Latino	Community Organizing/Education	Tepochcalli
Mayra	F	18	Latino	Community Organizing/Education	Tepochcalli
Henry	M	16	Latino	Community Organizing/Education	Tepochcalli
Esperanza	F	17	Latino	Community Organizing/Youth	Interfaith Leadership Project
Gisela	F	17	Latino	Community Organizing/Youth	Interfaith Leadership Project
Vianny	F	17	Latino	Community Organizing/Youth	Interfaith Leadership Project
Esshan	F	17	African American	Youth/Education	Southwest Youth Collaborative
Luis	M	16	Latino	Youth/Education	Southwest Youth Collaborative
Jo	F	16	African American	Youth/Education	Southwest Youth Collaborative
Jennifer	F	15	Latino	Youth/Education	Southwest Youth Collaborative
Wisdom	F	19	African American	Youth/Gender/Philanthropy	Girls' Best Friend
Sabura	F	16	African American	Youth/Gender/Philanthropy	Girls' Best Friend
Samantha	F	17	African American	Youth/Gender/Philanthropy	Girls' Best Friend
Noelle	F	17	African American	Writing/Youth Advocacy	Young Chicago Authors
Cristina	F	17	Latino	Writing/Youth Advocacy	Young Chicago Authors
David	M	16	White	Writing/Youth Advocacy	Young Chicago Authors
Jessie	M	17	Latino	Youth/Community Organizing Council	Brighton Park Youth
Daisy	F	19	Latino	Youth/Community Organizing Council	Brighton Park Youth
Terri	F	17	African American	Youth/Education Project	Multicultural Youth
Lindsey	F	16	White	Anti-War	Chicago Coalition Against the War
Carneil	M	16	African American	Electoral Activities/Debate	Mikva Challenge
Jessica	F	17	Latino	Electoral Activities/Debate	Mikva Challenge

Rio de Janeiro

Pseudonym	Gender	Age	Activities	Organization
Raquel	F	15	Participate in youth groups of political party, help organize political rallies, and recruit students	Juventude do PMDB [Youth of the Brazilian Democratic Party]
Denise	F	16	Dance, theater, and percussion to raise awareness of youth health issues	Caixa de Surpresa [Box of Surprise]
Marcia	F	16	Dance, theater, and percussion to raise awareness of youth health issues	Caixa de Surpresa [Box of Surprise]
Renato	M	16	Member of school council fighting for free bus passes and more university places for young people who attend government schools	Grêmio estudantil do Colégio Estadual Herbert de Souza [Student Association of Herbert de Souza State School]
Alexandra	F	17	Encourage other youth to attend church activities, assist in Sunday School classes, and distribute food baskets to the poor	Grupo Jovem Sementes de Afeto da Igreja Nossa Senhora da Lapa [Youth Group, the Seeds of Affection of Our Lady of Lapa]
Joana	F	17	Encourage other youth to attend church activities, assist in Sunday school classes, and distribute food baskets to the poor	Grupo jovem da Igreja Universal do Reino de Deus [Youth Group of the Universal Church of the Kingdom of God]
Lucas	M	17	Member of school council fighting for free bus passes and more university places for students who attend government schools	Grêmio estudantil do Colégio Estadual Herbert de Souza [Student Association of Herbert de Souza State School]
Leo	M	17	Youth organizer for children's rights	Juventude de Direitos Humanos—Projeto Legal [The Legal Project of the Youth for Human Rights]
Talita	F	18	Assist in center that exposes young slum children to reading and cultural activities	Centro de Educação e Cultura Lúdica da Rocinha [The Education and Play Culture Center of Rocinha]
Carla	F	20	Help run the press office of a political party in the "Indian Coast" of Brazil	Juventude do Partido da Frente Liberal (PFL) [Youth of the Liberal Front Party]
Felipe	M	19	Coach low-income high school students to pass university entrance exam	Projeto de Educação Comunitária da Escola Parque (PECEP) [Community Education Project of the Park School]

Name	Sex	Age	Activity	Organization
Jessica	F	18	Member of state student association fighting for student rights including free bus passes and more university places for students who attend government schools	Associação de Estudantes Secundaristas do Estado Rio de Janeiro (AERJ) [Secondary School Association of the State of Rio de Janeiro]; Grêmio Estudantil da Escola Prado Júnior [Student Association of the Prado Junior School]
Sabrina	F	18	Encourage other youth to attend church activities, give catechism classes, and distribute food baskets to the poor	Grupo Jovem da Igreja Nossa Senhora da Boa Viagem [Youth Group of Our Lady of the Good Voyage]
Luciano	M	20	Participate in youth groups of political party, help organize political rallies, and recruit students	Juventude Socialista do Partido Democrático Trabalhista (PDT) [Socialist Youth of the Democratic Workers' Party]
Jonas	M	20	Member of national and state associations fighting for student rights including free bus passes and more university places for students who attend government schools	União Brasileira dos Estudantes Secundaristas (UBES) [Brazilian National Students' Association]; Associação de Estudantes Secundaristas do Estado Rio de Janeiro (AERJ) [State of Rio de Janeiro Students Association]
Fatima	F	20	Participate in youth groups of political party, help organize political rallies, and recruit students	Juventude do Partido da Social Democracia Brasileira (PSDB) [Youth of the Brazilian Social Democratic Party]
Pedro	M	20	Member of national association fighting for student rights including free bus passes and more university places for students who attend government schools	União Brasileira dos Estudantes Secundarista (UBES) [Brazilian National Students' Association of the Brazilian Communist Party]
Miriam	F	20	Coach low-income high school students to pass university entrance exam	Pré-Vestibular Comunitário [Community Coaching for University Entrance Exams]; Jornal Comunitário Falando Alto [Community Newspaper Speaking Loudly]
Patricia	F	22	Use braids, crafts, handbags, and accessories to build young women's self-esteem	Ubuzima Grupo de Rap [Ubuzima Rap Group]

Rio de Janeiro (continued)

Pseudonym	Gender	Age	Activities	Organization
Gabriel	M	23	Help youth 16–24 to obtain workplace rights	Associação dos Adolescentes e Jovens Trabalhadores do Estado do Rio de Janeiro (AAJT/RJ) [Adolescent and Youth Workers Association of the State of Rio de Janeiro]
Fernando	M	24	Prepare programming for radio station whose goal is to support street children	Radio Madame Satã [Madam Satã Radio Group]
Jose	M	24	Carry out social programs to support youth in a low-income community	Projeto Bases de Apoio [Project Bases of Support]
Leonardo	M	24	Help organize the gay pride parade in Rio de Janeiro	Grupo Arco Íris de Conscientização Homossexual [Rainbow Group for Homosexual Consciousness]
Mateus	M	24	Training to obtain equity and rights for landless people, especially land redistribution	Movimento Sem Terra dos Trabalhadores Rurais (MST) [Landless Workers' Movement]

Mexico City

Pseudonym	Gender	Age	Activities	Organization
Julia	F	17	Participate in environmental protection campaigns	Greenpeace
Graciela	F	18	Participate in environmental protection campaigns	Greenpeace
Veronica	F	18	Participate in environmental protection campaigns	Greenpeace
Nora	F	13	Promote children's rights among schoolmates and in other public schools of the municipality	Red Nacional de DIF-usores infantiles [Children's National Network for the Promotion of Rights]—Cuauhtemoc Municipality

Name	Gender	Age	Role	Organization
Miriam	F	16	Promote children's rights among schoolmates and in other public schools of the municipality	Red Nacional de DIF—usores infantiles [Children's National Network for the Promotion of Rights]—Cuauhtemoc Municipality
Enrique	M	16	Participate in group performances and other artistic multimedia projects that involve other youth organizations in low-economic urban cultural centers	Machincuepa—Social Circus Project
Monica	F	15	Participate in group performances and other artistic multimedia projects that involve other youth organizations in low-economic urban cultural centers	Machincuepa—Social Circus Project
Nestor	M	15	Participate in group performances and other artistic multimedia projects that involve other youth organizations in low-economic urban cultural centers	Machincuepa—Social Circus Project
Jimena	F	17	Participate in group performances and other artistic multimedia projects that involve other youth organizations in low-economic urban cultural centers	Machincuepa—Social Circus Project
Javier	M	18	Participate in group performances and other artistic multimedia projects that involve other youth organizations in low-economic urban cultural centers	Machincuepa—Social Circus Project
Juan	M	24	Participate in group performances; promote and direct conjoint artistic projects that involve other youth organizations in low-economic urban cultural centers	Machincuepa—Social Circus Project/ Ixtehuan—Community video project
Horacio	M	19	Coach children and adolescents in summer camps for disadvantaged children	Colonias de Vacaciones [Summer Camps Program]
Basilio	M	18	Participate and promote activities among youth related to international intercultural youth exchanges	AFS Intercultural Programs

Mexico City (*continued*)

Pseudonym	Gender	Age	Activities	Organization
Lilia	F	15	Participate in the production, editing, and creation of multimedia video projects with a social content	Ixtehuan—Community video project
Camila	F	16	Participate in the production, editing, and creation of multimedia video projects with a social content	Ixtehuan—Community video project
Alejandro	M	16	Participate in the production, editing, and creation of multimedia video projects with a social content	Ixtehuan—Community video project
Fernando	M	17	Member of board of the organization; promotion, organization, and participation in family planning and reproductive health campaigns among youth with a genre and human rights perspective	Mexfam [Mexican Foundation for Family Planning]
Carlos	M	17	Participate in the production, editing, and creation of multimedia video projects with a social content	Video Activo
Genaro	M	19	Founder of the organization to promote youth political participation; director of a radio Internet program on social and political issues targeted to youth audience	Causa Joven [Youth Cause]
Antonio	M	23	Founder and director of the organization to promote cultural, social, and sports activities among low-income youth; offer reproductive health and drug addiction prevention courses to secondary schools	Tepocatl
Lucia	F	20	Organize youth forums to promote social participation and youth projects	Se Lider
Susana	F	20	Founder and director of the organization; get funding, organize youth forums to promote social participation and youth projects	Se Lider

Index

Page numbers in **boldface** refer to illustrations.

Gabriel (youth activist, Rio de Janeiro), 70–71, 83
gay rights, 70, 76, 79, 101, 111
Genaro (youth activist, Mexico City), 108, 114
gender: awareness of, as social identity, 40; discrimination and, 43; identity and, 41–42; representation of, by youth activists, 45; social participation and, 63; urban youth in U.S. and, 10; violence in Mexico City and, 19; young boys, 93, 99–100; of youth activists in Chicago, 31. *See also* women
generational engagement, 2
Girl's Best Friend Foundation (Chicago), 30, 47
Gisela (youth activist, Chicago), 36, 41, 42, 43, 52
global awareness of young activists, 56–57, 111, 133, 140
globalization, 6–7, 133; economic restructuring and, 12; nation-states and, 15
government: activism aimed at, 130–31; young activists' ideals of, 54–56, 138
governmental organizations, 2
Graciela (youth activist, Mexico City), 93, 96, 97, 116
grassroots organizations, 2. *See also* community organizations
Greenpeace: members of, 92, 93, 96, 99, 102, 114
Guantanamo Base, Cuba, 7

helping (term): political meaning of, 69, 139
Henry (youth activist, Chicago), 32–33, 36, 43, 44, 48
history, importance of, 113
HIV information, 111
homicide rates: in Brazil, 18, 61–62; in Mexico City, 19
Horacio (youth activist, Mexico City), 98, 99, 105
human connections: foreign policy and, 56
Human Development Index (HDI), 91
human rights, 91

IBASE (Brazilian Institute for Social and Economic Analyses), 9, 63–64
identities: awareness of, 40–41, 126–28, 139–40; discrimination and, 42–45;

engagement and, 16; national identity, 43, 112–13, 126, 127; of youth, 10
identity politics, 39–40, 126–27
immigrant parents, 34–36
immigrants: in Chicago, 29–30; discrimination against, 43–44, 50–51; importance of, 50, 55; inclusivity desired by, 138
immigration reform, 2, 50–51, 133
inclusivity, 138, 140
income inequality, 62. *See also* poverty
independence, 12
indigenous youth, 5, 94, 95, 101–2, 105, 111
inequalities: in Brazil, 62; in Chicago, 18; economic, 6; in education, 46–47; education as source of, 84, 129; in Mexico, 90–91; in Mexico City, 18; in Rio de Janeiro, 18
insecurity, 93
Institute for Religious Studies (ISER) (Brazil), 9, 63
Institute for Studies, Training, and the Consultancy in Social Policies (IBASE and Instituto Pólis), 9
Institutional Revolutionary Party (PRI) (Mexico), 19, 90, 129, 130
Instituto Pólis (Brazil), 9, 63
Interfaith Leadership Project (Chicago), 30, 38; members of, 34, 36, 41
Internet, the, 110
Iraq War (2003–2011), 36, 51–52, 133
Ixtehuan (Mexico City), 102; members of, 93, 96, 110

Javier (youth activist, Mexico City), 96–97, 99–100
Jennifer (youth activist, Chicago), 32, 36, 37, 41, 43, 45, 47, 56, 57
Jesse (youth activist, Chicago), 33, 38
Jessica (youth activist, Chicago), 31–32, 34, 36, 37, 41, 48, 55, 57
Jessica (youth activist, Rio de Janeiro), 67, 78, 81–82, 83–84
Jimena (youth activist, Mexico City), 96, 98, 106, 107
Jo (youth activist, Chicago), 33, 38, 40, 57
Joana (youth activist, Rio de Janeiro), 67, 80
Jonas (youth activist, Rio de Janeiro), 68, 70, 73, 78, 79, 82, 85

The Young People of Rio: Paths, Beliefs and Approaches (study), 80
youth: definitions of, 10–12, 91; discrimination against, 42, 126; diversity of, 67, 126; as political category, 4, 128, 139–40; power of, 40; representation of, by youth activists, 44–45
youth activism: transgressive view of, 8
youth activists: as agents of change vs. model citizens, 4; Brazilian, **3**; families of, 122–23; influences on, 122–25; mid-twentieth century emergence of, 4; personal characteristics of, 125–26, 132; political ideas of, 135–40; responsibilities of, 125–26; social awareness of, 125–28; social identities of, 126–28
youth activists, in Chicago, Illinois, 31–57; demographics of, 31; families of, 34–36; identities of, 126–27; influences on, 33–39; issues important to, 45–52, 129; political ideas of, 52–57, 138; religion and, 125; responsibilities of, 31–33, 44–45, 126; self-perceptions of, 31–32; social awareness of, 39–45; youth rights awareness of, 137
youth activists, in Mexico City, Mexico, 92–118; critical experiences of, 106–7; demographics of, 92–94; educational trajectories of, 94–95, 129–30; engagement of, 107–11; families of, 93–94, 99–101; identity of, 112–13, 126; influences on, 99–107; motivations for involvement of, 105–7; organizations involved in, 94; personal characteristics

of, 95–97; political ideas of, 112–17, 138; religion and, 97–98, 125; responsibilities of, 99, 126; social status and, 96; technology and, 131–32; youth rights awareness of, 136, 137
youth activists, in Rio de Janeiro, Brazil, 63–88; activities involved in, 74–77; altruism of, 139; degrees of involvement of, 77–78; demographics of, 65–66; identity and, 126; influences on, 67–74; involved with student movement, 124; issues important to, 84–87, 129; motivations for engagement of, 69–71; natural inclinations of, 67–68; political ideas of, 78–84, 138; religion and, 125; responsibilities of, 74, 77, 85–87, 125; youth rights awareness of, 136–37
Youth and Young People: What Unites Them and What Separates Them? (UNESCO study), 64–65
youth empowerment: importance of families in, 141–42; through organizational involvement, 37–38, 38–39; social stigma as source of, 111, 127; of women, 124–25
youth engagement studies, 7–9
Youth of the Brazilian Democratic Party, 72
youth rights: awareness of, 136–37; in Brazil, 6
yo-yo trajectory, 95

zero tolerance rule, 47

MARIA DE LOS ANGELES TORRES is director and professor of Latin American and Latin studies at the University of Illinois at Chicago. **IRENE RIZZINI** is a professor at the Pontifical Catholic University of Rio de Janeiro, Brazil, and the director of the International Center for Research on Childhood. **NORMA DEL RÍO** is a professor of psychology in the department of education and communication at the Metropolitan Autonomous University–Cochimilco (UAM) in Mexico City.

The University of Illinois Press
is a founding member of the
Association of American University Presses.

Composed in 9/13 ITC Stone Serif
with ITC Stone Sans display
by Lisa Connery
at the University of Illinois Press
Manufactured by Thomson-Shore, Inc.

University of Illinois Press
1325 South Oak Street
Champaign, IL 61820-6903
www.press.uillinois.edu